ANCIENT IRISH MONUMENTS

Ancient Irish Monuments

PETER HARBISON

Gill & Macmillan

Gill & Macmillan Ltd
Goldenbridge
Dublin 8
with associated companies throughout the world
© Peter Harbison 1997
0 7171 2534 3

The moral right of the author has been asserted.

Index compiled by Helen Litton
Illustrations by Hilary Gilmore
Original text design by Identikit Design Consultants, Dublin
Print origination by Carole Lynch
Printed by ColourBooks Ltd, Dublin

This book is typeset in 10/15 pt Bembo.

A catalogue record is available for this book
from the British Library.

1 3 5 4 2

The extract from 'Who Will Solve It' is taken from
Colony and Frontier in Medieval Ireland: Essays Presented
to J. F. Lydon (The Hambledon Press, 1995) and is used with
the permission of the poet, Brendan Kennelly.

Our thanks to Malachy McCloskey and
Jacqueline O'Brien for help with illustrations.

Contents

Introduction   7
Time Chart   8

Passage-graves   9
Dolmens   14
Stone Circles   16
Celtic Decorated Stones   20
Earthen and Stone 'Forts'   22
Ogham   26
Early Monasteries   28
Corbelled Huts and Oratories   33
Cross-decorated Stones   37
High Crosses   40
Round Towers   45
Romanesque Churches   49
Cistercian Abbeys   53
Medieval Cathedrals   58
Norman Castles   62
Medieval Walled Towns   66
Effigies of Knights, Ladies and Bishops   70
Medieval Domestic Buildings   74
Medieval Friaries   78
Tower-houses   83
Plantation Castles   87
Post-medieval Fortifications   91

Bibliography   93
Index to Place Names   94

Round Tower, Timahoe, Co. Laois

Introduction

I dream the dead into a living presence
and shape dead bones into a new design,
let speak again the ages' buried voices
and so defy the killing power of time.

These imaginative words by the poet Brendan Kennelly, penned in honour of the historian J. F. Lydon, encapsulate why it is worth studying Ireland's ancient monuments — to bring the dead to life through what they created, and to let the mute stones speak.

Ireland has a great variety of ancient monuments, and various types are discussed here in succession so as to give young and old, Irish and visitor, an idea of the rich heritage in stone which the country possesses. This book is designed to introduce the interested traveller to these ancient stones, so that he or she may have a heightened appreciation when they see them standing proudly in the Irish countryside on sites where they have survived the wind and rain for upwards of five hundred years and more.

Tall Cross,
Monasterboice,
Co. Louth

TIME CHART

| | 3000 B.C. | 2000 B.C. | 1000 B.C. | B.C. A.D. | A.D. 1000 | A.D. 2000 |

Passage-graves
Dolmens
Stone circles
Celtic decorated stones
Earthen and stone 'forts'
Ogham
Early monasteries
Corbelled huts and oratories
Cross-decorated stones
High crosses
Round towers
Romanesque churches
Cistercian abbeys
Medieval cathedrals
Norman castles
Medieval walled towns
Effigies of knights, ladies and bishops
Medieval domestic buildings
Medieval friaries
Tower-houses
Plantation castles
Post-medieval fortifications

N.B. The periods should be taken as approximate rather than absolute.

Passage-graves

Of all the various kinds of Stone Age megalithic tombs in Ireland, the passage-grave or passage-tomb is by far the most dominant. Its builders sought out prominent hilltop sites which could be seen from a distance, so that the population living on the plains below could — in more senses than one — look up to those who were laid to rest in these lofty graves, for it was they who had probably created the surplus wealth which made it possible to build such conspicuous monuments. These tombs were contained in a large dome-shaped cairn — a mound of stone and earth — sometimes delimited by a stone kerb, and with a passage leading from the perimeter into a burial chamber at or near the centre of the tumulus.

By far the most famous passage-graves in Ireland are the trio located in the sacred landscape of the Boyne Valley — Newgrange, Knowth and Dowth — all sited on a series of low hills some miles upstream from Drogheda. Newgrange has become one of Europe's most renowned prehistoric monuments because of the interest created by the sun shining into the darkest recesses of the tomb on the shortest day of the year (and on a few days on either side of it) for a mere seventeen minutes, before it quietly exits for another year. The simple message which this eerily calculated happening was designed to leave behind was that there is a life after death, in the same way that the sun breathes new life into nature's annual cycle after the nadir it experiences in the depths of winter. The intentional orientation of the passage towards the point on the horizon where the sun rises at the winter solstice, the clever method used to allow the sun's rays to enter the

mound above the entrance doorway before penetrating
through to the tomb centre, and the ingenious corbel
construction of the burial chamber roof which still keeps
the interior as dry as a bone after five thousand years —
not to mention the marvellous decoration both within and
outside the tomb — all show that passage-tombs like this
were built by an extremely clever and highly sophisticated
people. We cannot but stand in awe of their brilliant use
of whatever simple Stone Age technology was at their
disposal to construct a masterpiece like Newgrange —
one of the world's first great pieces of architecture, and
a prodigy which is probably some centuries older than
the pyramids of Egypt.

The geometrical decoration of spirals, lozenges and
other curious shapes at Newgrange are found in other
passage-graves, including its near neighbour Knowth,
where many of the kerbstones surrounding the great
mound are decorated with a variety of motifs, as are the
inaccessible tombs within — for Knowth is remarkable for
having two known passage-graves within a single mound.
There was doubtless a symbolism behind the designs used
on these stones, but its meaning still remains beyond our
ken despite the numerous and ingenious attempts to
decode it. Yet it is perhaps not too fanciful to see the
angular and curvilinear motifs as having been imitated
from patterns — on wood or woven tapestries? — which
decorated the long-disintegrated houses of the living, so as
to make the dead in the tombs feel more at home, as it
were. Could it even be that the combination of motifs,
which varies from tomb to tomb, might represent the
emblem of the particular family whose burial vault the
passage-grave was, like a Scots tartan or the patterns of an
Aran Island sweater?

One motif, easily recognisable in its various manifestations, is particularly popular in another of the great passage-grave cemeteries in County Meath, that at Lough Crew near Oldcastle. This is the sun, shown as a disc with lines radiating out from it. The repetition there of this obvious solar symbol would support the notion that the sun must have been the most important — and perhaps even the sole — god in the passage-grave pantheon, an inference which could obviously be drawn equally at Newgrange. Fourknocks, the most southerly of County Meath's passage-graves, close to the Dublin border, is the only tomb of its kind to show a clearly recognisable human figure among its ornamented stones, and the infectious smile on its face carries a mirthful message across the centuries to such an extent that its original discoverer dubbed it 'The Jester' — though we still do not know what it was he was smiling about. Like the rest of passage-grave art — and Chesterton's donkey — it keeps its secret still.

Decorated stones also occur on other passage-graves too, as on Seefin Mountain in County Wicklow and Knockmany near Augher in County Tyrone. The other great concentration of passage-graves, in County Sligo, was for long thought to have lacked decoration, but one clear example has recently been located at tomb 51 — known locally as Listoghil — in the great cemetery at Carrowmore not far from Sligo town. This was once one of the largest cemeteries of megalithic tombs in the whole of Europe, but it is sadly much depleted now through gravel digging during the last century and a half.

Carrowmore is a rather unusual cemetery in that some of its tombs have central chambers with a passage which does not necessarily extend out to the round

monument's edge, which is delineated by a circle of
stones. The same feature is also found at Knockmany,
mentioned above, but may also have been present in
the impressive 'Stone Circle' (so called) at Beltany in
County Donegal. But other Carrowmore monuments
have a dolmen within a circle of stones, and, when
excavated, these tombs produced finds of mushroom-
headed bone pins and chalk balls so similar to those
found in other passage-tombs that they too should be
included under the broad umbrella term of passage-tomb.
Looking down benignly on Carrowmore is the great
mound known as Queen Medhbh's (or Maeve's) Grave
on top of Knocknarea, offering an unrivalled view of
much of Sligo's coastline. It is probably the largest
unopened passage-grave in Ireland, though without
excavation it is, of course, impossible to be sure, and
it does have the distinction of featuring in Yeats's
famous couplet:

> *The wind has bundled up the clouds high*
> *over Knocknarea*
> *And thrown the thunder on the stones for all*
> *that Maeve can say.*

Slightly smaller, though no less significant, humps on
the Sligo skyline are the series of passage-graves on the
mountain at Carrowkeel, overlooking Lough Arrow.
These were 'excavated' over a period of little more than
a fortnight in 1911 and proved to be 'classic' passage-
graves having passages and well-built chambers with a
cruciform ground plan like Newgrange, though one was
more in the shape of a double-armed cross, created by
the addition of a second set of side chambers.

For long the great tumuli of the Boyne Valley were
regarded as the first and greatest of the passage-tombs,
and were subsequently dated by radiocarbon methods to
around 3000 B.C. But similar methods produced calibrated
radiocarbon dates for the Carrowmore Cemetery which
were up to a thousand and more years earlier and, though
still controversial, they could be seen as arguing in favour
of seeing this County Sligo necropolis as being earlier than
Newgrange and Knowth. If this be correct, we should
then see the great Boyne Valley tombs not as being among
the first, but among the last and greatest expression of
passage-grave construction, the zenith and culmination of
up to a thousand years of experimentation. But no matter
when these remarkable tombs were built, they evince an
awe-inspiring respect for the housing of the dead, in
contrast to the huts of those who built the tombs, which
were of much more ephemeral construction and have since
almost totally disappeared to such an extent that we cannot
even locate their whereabouts.

Stone Circle, Carrowmore, Co. Sligo

Dolmens

Among Ireland's many megalithic tombs, the dolmens may be classed as among the most lovable, for they are small yet impressive and visually very stimulating. They were also among the first to appeal to the interests of the dilettanti archaeologists of the eighteenth century, who saw in them altars on which the ancient druids would have made sacrifices. The name itself is not too far removed from this concept, as it is derived from two Breton words meaning a 'stone table'.

We have already come across them at Carrowmore in County Sligo, sometimes forming the focus of a stone circle, at other times standing on their own. There, they can be very low on the ground — looking not much larger than a giant tortoise with stumpy legs carrying its covering on its back, for dolmens usually consist of between three and seven legs carrying one or two capstones on top. But others, at Carrowmore and elsewhere, stand higher off the ground, reaching a height of 10 feet (3.3m) at Aughnacliff, Co. Longford, and 13 feet (4m) at Proleek in County Louth. The very shape of a few uprights carrying a large capstone can lead to striking visual comparisons — images of a bird about to take off (not to mention a Concorde aeroplane) at Kilclooney, Co. Donegal, or a coffin on stilts, as at Legananny, Co. Down. One learned Cambridge professor described dolmens as being among the earliest pieces of public sculpture anywhere in Europe — and not without some justification.

Though folklore sees them as the beds of the romantic lovers Diarmuid and Gráinne, the more down to earth

truth revealed by excavation is that these dolmens were
tombs for the Stone Age dead, a chamber for their mortal
remains usually separated from the outside world by a
stone blocking the entrance to the tombs. Not many
dolmens have, in fact, been excavated, and even fewer
have provided information which helps to place them in
some comprehensive prehistoric context, but one of the
most valuable of these is also one of the most
photographed dolmens — Poulnabrone on the limestone
plateau of the Burren in County Clare. Here, bones of
between 16 and 22 individuals of both sexes were
discovered in a jumbled condition, suggesting that the
dead may have been exposed for defleshing — presumably
by birds — before their bones were finally laid to rest, the
bones of ancestors probably having been seen as providing
legitimation for the ownership of land. One hip bone
found in the excavation of Poulnabrone still contained an
arrow-head buried in the tomb with its victim sometime
between 3800 and 3200 B.C. Other finds included a stone
axe, quartz crystals and a mushroom-headed bone pin.
Around the tomb were the remnants of a mound of stones
less than two feet in height — scarcely tall enough to have
been a denuded cairn which would once have covered the
dolmen, giving support to the Cambridge professor's
notion of the upright stones having been intended from
the start as a starkly sculptural form against the skyline.
But some kind of ramp must once have existed, because
how could we otherwise contemplate Stone Age man,
without any block and tackle, succeeding in levering
a 50-ton capstone into position on top of the uprights so
that it would retain its balance for five thousand years —
and hopefully very much longer.

Stone Circles

O nce upon a time, a piper went out to play with a group of young people who were intent on amusing themselves by dancing. But, because it was a sabbath that they had chosen for their céilí, the Lord picked the moment when the dancers were pirouetting around in a circle to turn them all into stone as a punishment. This story, which gave its name to two stone circles in County Wicklow — The Piper's Stones — obviously stems from the puritanical days of the seventeenth century, and was probably introduced into Ireland from somewhere on the far side of the Irish Sea, where it is also recorded. The piper comes into the story because, outside some Irish stone circles, there is a tall and separate stone — 'The Piper' — standing by itself, the original function of which can only be guessed at with difficulty.

Another Wicklow folk story, however, also associates the stones with music and musicians. According to this, the Piper's Stones, at Brewel near Dunlavin, came into existence because three musicians, who were vying with one another as to who could throw a stone the furthest, each tossed his stone on to the side of a nearby hill, but an ambitious young piper who wanted to flaunt his prowess in front of his older colleagues only managed to have his stone land behind the others.

Another tale in a different part of the country brings us back into a deeper prehistoric past. Sir William Wilde, antiquarian and father of Oscar, recorded that, near Cong in County Mayo, there is a circle which is associated with the mythical Battle of Moytura which is said to have been fought long before St Patrick ever ventured across the Irish horizon. One of those present was a man thought to have been Balor, who used to melt his enemies with the evil eye at the back of his head. To get the better of him, his adversaries erected the stone circle and painted the stones with figures of warriors, and when Balor saw that his eye power was having no effect, he retreated in confusion. Further south, at Grange, near Lough Gur in County Limerick, one of the largest of Ireland's stone circles is traditionally attributed to Crom Dubh, a little black(-haired) man who is credited with having brought the first sheaf of wheat to Ireland.

And who are we to know better? Perhaps this old tradition is not too far wide of the mark, for the stone circles in Ireland may have been built by Stone Age farmers around the fourth millennium B.C., and the Grange Stone Circle has been ascribed to the Late Stone Age, perhaps sometime around 3000 B.C. The circles vary considerably in size, as they may also have done in function. One of the smallest is an embanked circle at Lissyvigeen outside Killarney which consists of seven stones with a diameter of only about 12 feet (4m). In contrast, the largest stone circle in the country is that surrounding the great passage-grave at Newgrange which has a diameter of 340 feet (103.6m), but only twelve out of an estimated original number of 35 stones still survive from the circle. For many a visitor to Newgrange, these massive roughly-hewn stones — which are such a noticeable feature outside the entrance to the grave — seem to be a natural part of the tomb complex, acting like a belt to hold it together and allow access to and from the outside world. But excavation proved that these stones were put up around the outside of the great burial mound about a thousand years after it was built, and possibly even

by a totally different people from those who had erected
the passage-tomb.

Another very large circle, enclosing what may really
have been a passage-tomb or round cairn, is Beltany stone
circle in County Donegal which has a diameter of over
156 feet (47.5m) and still preserves 64 out of an estimated
80 of its stones, one marked with small hemispherical
hollows known as cup-marks. Further links between
stone circles and megalithic tombs are provided in the
great cemetery at Carrowmore, Co. Sligo, where the
circles can be seen to enclose dolmens, among others.

In some of the smaller examples which are not in any
way associated with megalithic tombs, a horizontally laid
stone can be seen occasionally placed diagonally opposite
another which may be taller than the rest, and if a line be
drawn between the two and continued to the horizon,
it may indicate a place where the sun may rise or set on
some significant day in the annual calendar — such as an
equinox or solstice, the beginning of spring or 1 May.
One example where this has been seen to be the case is
Drombeg, serenely sited in the rolling pastoral landscape
of west Cork. Here, for a few days at and on either side
of the shortest day of the year, the sun can be seen to
set close to a noticeable V-shaped gap in the horizon
to the west.

Such observations have led to the not unjustified
speculation that particular stones in the circle were given
prominence because they were used to help mark the
progress of the sun at particular times of the year. But to
do so in this way would surely only have required just two
stones to form a sight line which could be continued to
the horizon at a point where the sun rose or set on very
special days. So, could the whole circle have been created,

then, to offer a place of worship to the sun god, its round shape imitating the orb of the sun, which must surely have been the god of some of the megalith builders? Given the old folklore traditions associating music with these circles, it would not be surprising if some of the ceremonies that took place within the circle were accompanied by some form of musical manifestation.

Stone circles occur in widely differing parts of the country. Wicklow has already been mentioned, and Lissyvigeen is only one of many circles in the Cork–Kerry area. These are often attractively sited, as is the case at Drombeg, but also Kealkil in County Cork, which has a view down a valley towards Bantry Bay. But another important cluster is found stretching across the whole of northern Ireland, with the largest grouping by far being at Beaghmore, near Cookstown in County Tyrone, where nine circles have been recovered from beneath the surface of the bog. Excavations at a number of circles from Drombeg in County Cork to Beaghmore, as well as at Ballynoe in County Down, have helped to show that stone circles may have had a long life stretching over hundreds, if not thousands, of years, from the end of the Stone Age to well on into the Bronze Age — but not, apparently, into the Iron Age after 500 B.C., as had for long been thought to have been the case with Drombeg.

But for all the research that has been done on stone circles, they leave open the intriguing question as to what they were built for, and what they achieved. For a long time to come, one suspects they will continue to tickle our curiosity and set our minds to imaginative flights of fancy, but will ultimately keep us guessing.

Celtic Decorated Stones

T he physical remains of the ancient Celts all over
Europe show these people to have been great masters
of the decorative arts in a variety of media. To see
that, all you need to do is to go and see the Iron Age
metalwork in the National Museum of Ireland in Dublin.
But the Celts have also left us proof of their mastery in
stone as well, even if the surviving examples are not as
numerous as we might wish. But each one is an enigma
in itself.

The most famous is that at Turoe in County Galway,
close to the village of Bullaun, not far from Loughrea.
It is a cylindrical granite boulder, domed on top and
decorated with a stepped motif of Greek ancestry, above
which is a beautiful collection of swirling motifs of Celtic
genius. These go in and out like the ebb and flow of the
tide, some looking like a trumpet end and one even like
the stylised head of a bird. When analysed, the whole
composition can be broken down into four individual
fields, suggesting that the design was copied from one
used on a four-sided (pyramidal?) object, perhaps of wood.
What was the purpose of such a stone? The archaeologist
would say 'ritual' because he cannot be more precise.
But this is where we have to let our imagination come
into play — could the four 'sides' have had something to
do with the corners of the earth? Could the Turoe stone,
which was originally located at a rath or ring-fort a few
miles away, have been seen as some kind of earth centre —
or was it an elaborately ornamented phallic symbol? We
shall probably never know; it is probably better that way,
as it is always much more interesting to keep guessing!

The same mystery applies to its siblings which are spread over various parts of Ireland. Its nearest counterpart is a rather smaller version at Castlestrange in County Roscommon, while others of somewhat different appearance are now preserved in museums — one from Killycluggin, Co. Cavan, in the National Museum in Dublin, and another from Derrykeighan, Co. Antrim, now in the Ulster Museum in Belfast — these last two clearly having had their motifs designed with the aid of a compass.

Celtic stones of a very different kind are the figure sculptures on two separate islands in Lough Erne. The first of these is in Caldragh cemetery on Boa Island, where two figures, back to back with one another, are carved on the same stone, with a small cavity on top between their heads. They have been likened to the Roman Janus idols.

Not far away is White Island, close to Castle Archdale and reachable from the marina there. Standing within an enclosure on the islet is a ruined Romanesque church, and built into one of its interior walls is a curious collection of figures which stand out in high relief. One bears two quadrupeds with bird-like beaks sniffing one another; a second has its hands in a muffler; a third sits bemused and cross legged; a fourth holds a staff and a bell; and a fifth a sword and a shield. This last warrior figure wears a penannular brooch which helps to date the whole group to around A.D. 800 — making them clearly Christian, not pagan. But what does this strange collection of figures represent? More pointedly, why was such a curious assemblage brought together, and for what purpose? The quizzical expressions on their faces look as if they will keep us searching for answers to these questions for many centuries to come.

Earthen and Stone 'Forts'

After the word *Baile* (anglicised Bally) meaning a
settlement or hamlet, some of the most common
elements in Irish placenames include *Rath*, *Lios* or
Lis, *Dún*, *Caishel* (Cashel) and *Cathair*. All of these words
suggest some sense of defence in the type of settlement
they denote, which are frequently bundled together
under the general umbrella term of 'ring-fort'. These
consist essentially of a round wall of earth or stone, often
with a ditch outside, and having a diameter varying
between 50 and 115 feet (15 and 35m). Yet it is really
something of a misnomer to have the word 'fort'
included in their label, as this implies an area defended by
a garrison, however small. In reality, a ring-fort probably
contained little more than a single family unit and its
retainers, who could not realistically have expected to
defend such a ring-fort in the face of any determined
attack. A ring-fort can then probably be best compared to
its latter-day counterpart, the country house or cottage,
surrounded by its fence or garden hedge, with the
circular earthwork having acted as the fence to keep
animals in at night, while the area within the circular
earthwork would have contained a house or houses so
flimsy as to have long since disappeared without trace.
It was in order to help our imagination in visualising
what a ring-fort looked like that the late John Hunt
reconstructed one at Craggaunowen in County Clare in
the 1970s, and similar aids to understanding history have
been launched in the meantime at Ferrycarrig in County
Wexford and in the Ulster History Park near Omagh,
County Tyrone.

The various different names for what seems like
the single 'ring-fort' concept did, however, have separate
meanings originally. *Rath* at first denoted just the circular
earthen wall, but later came to include the whole area it
enclosed, and this is the sense in which the word *rath* is
widely used today. In that, it is almost interchangeable
with the word *lios* (or *lis*) which, however, originally
signified the open area between the earthen wall and the
house within its enclosure, but there is also a geographical
difference in the distribution of the two words, *rath* being
more common in Leinster, whereas *lios* predominates
outside the province.

The same can also be said of the two words denoting
the stone fort — *caiseal* being common in the north-west,
whereas *cathair* (or caher) is more frequent in the west and
south-west. Both indicate the major distribution area of
stone forts which are found in the stony areas of the
western half of Ireland from Kerry to Donegal. These
can be fully circular walls, as at Staigue Fort in Kerry or
the Grianán of Aileach in County Donegal, both of which
have massive walls reaching to a height of almost 20 feet
(6.5m). Typical of both of these forts — one located in a
lonesome valley, the other on a hilltop with a splendid
panorama over Loughs Foyle and Swilly — is the slightly
sloping external wall and the criss-crossing steps leading
to a parapet on its inner face. But this, too, is exactly what
we find in the stone forts of the Aran Islands, of which
the best known by far is Dún Aengus, perched on a rock
ledge which falls sheer almost 200 feet (65m) to the
Atlantic Ocean below. It, however, is approximately
semicircular in shape, not because half of it has collapsed
into the sea, but because its builders cleverly used the
unclimbable cliff face as a natural defence to save them

having to build the other half. In a similar instance, at
Cahercommaun in the Burren area of north Clare, the
builders flattened one side of the circle on a cliff face,
again to save themselves the bother. But the builders of
Dún Aengus gave themselves a lot of additional work by
placing upright stones close together outside one of the
walls in what is known as *chevaux-de-frise*. Designed to
make approach difficult for an attacker, this form of
defence was also used at another, smaller, round fort in
County Clare — Caherballykinvarga, near Kilfenora —
but also on a promontory fort known as Dubh Cathair, on
Inis Mór, the largest of the Aran Islands in Galway Bay.

Tradition says that these stone forts on the Aran
Islands were built by the Fir Bolg, a somewhat mythical
people (though probably associated with the Belgae whom
Caesar encountered on the European continent) who, it
was said, arrived on the east coast of Ireland and, after
refusing to pay their taxes there, were pushed westwards
until they could go no further — and so they stayed on
the Aran Islands.

The *rath* and the *lios* are, with few exceptions, datable
to around the first millennium of the Christian era,
though some were used, and possibly even built, after
the arrival of the Normans. But the dating of their stone
counterparts, the cashels and the cahers, is altogether more
problematical. Recent excavations at Dún Aengus suggest
at least that some of the walls were built as early as the
Late Bronze Age, say, around 800–700 B.C. and possibly
earlier. A 1930s dig at Cahercommaun produced a
beautiful silver brooch dating from around the eighth
century A.D., but as it may have belonged, not to the
original builders, but rather to later intruders who could
have hidden it there, the caher may be considerably older.

Another stone fort not far away in the Burren, namely Cahermacnaghten, was occupied by a legal family at least until the seventeenth century, but precisely when it was built is anybody's guess. The use and construction of both earthen and stone forts over at least one millennium, and quite possibly two, helps to make them the most common field monument of ancient Ireland, the total number of ring-forts having been estimated in the last century to have been around 30,000. But many of these have sadly fallen prey in the meantime to modern agricultural development. It is much to be regretted that the fairies, who were so successful in protecting them against destruction in the past, have not been winning the battle against the modern mechanical earth-mover.

Craggaunowen Stone Fort, Co. Clare

Ogham

Ogham is an alphabet or cypher system which bears the oldest known inscriptions in the Irish language. It is made up of anything between one and five notches which are engraved on, diagonally across, or on either side of a central line, providing a total of 20 signs (19 letters of our own alphabet and the diphthong NG). With the exception of a few examples in medieval manuscripts, ogham writing survives almost exclusively on upright stones, one sharper edge of which acts as the central line for purposes of the inscription. Where comprehensible, the text says something like 'of A son of B' or 'X descendant of Y' — and little more. None of the names mentioned on the ogham stones has ever been satisfactorily equated with that of any known historical personage.

The stones may well have acted as memorials to those whose names are carved on them, and this is the function ascribed to ogham stones in the old Irish sagas. But the same tales also tell how messages in ogham were carved in wood, and even scratched in iron, which can in no way be construed as memorials. One instance of this was when Cú Chulainn, the great young Irish hero, sent a threatening challenge to his opponents — written in ogham on a wooden hoop.

It is, indeed, quite likely that ogham developed in a medium such as wood rather than in stone, but where and how this happened has been a matter of much debate for centuries. That it was based on the Roman alphabet is very probable, and those who developed ogham are most likely to have come into contact with Roman lettering in

western Britain where some ogham inscriptions still
survive. Ogham is likely to have been practised at least as
far back as the fourth century A.D., if not earlier, so that
its earliest use in Ireland may, therefore, have been in a
purely pagan context. However, it must have continued
in practical use for a number of centuries, and even
survived as an academic exercise until little more than
a hundred years ago.

Quite a number of ogham stones have a Christian
context, being found on a number of old monastic sites
such as Ardfert in County Kerry and Ardmore, Co.
Waterford. Some ogham inscriptions share a stone with an
incised cross which, in the case of one example from
Church Island in County Kerry (now preserved in Cork
Public Museum), can be shown to have been earlier
than the ogham.

While found scattered in many parts of Ireland,
there is a notable concentration of ogham stones in
Counties Cork, Kerry and Waterford. No particularly
satisfactory reason is forthcoming to explain this
distribution, but these are certainly areas where ogham
stones are best sought out — along with the National
Museum and the collection in the cloisters of
University College, Cork.

In Waterford, ogham stones were found making up
roofing stones for a souterrain or underground passage at
Drumlohan, and others which served a similar function
were salvaged and placed in a semicircle at Dunloe, near
Killarney. It is further west, in the Iveragh and Dingle
Peninsulas, that one of the country's largest collection
of ogham stones is to be found, including that at
Kilmalkedar, north of Dingle.

Early Monasteries

We owe a great debt of gratitude to the monasteries which started to mushroom over many parts of Ireland from the sixth century onwards. They helped to keep alight the flame of Christianity introduced by St Patrick — and probably by others before him — and developed an ascetic lifestyle which made some Irish monks and hermits role models for the rest of Europe.

Coming into existence when paganism was still a force to be reckoned with, the monasteries were sufficiently liberal of intellect to gather the store of lore which had come down by word of mouth from generations of heathen Celts, and subsequently to write it down in great manuscript codices which happily survive to our own day. Without the monkish scribes we would know little or nothing of Cú Chulainn and the Red Branch knights or of the exploits of Finn and the Fianna, not to mention the great corpus of old Irish literature, laws and poetry, which would otherwise have been lost to us.

The monasteries also fostered the art of manuscript illumination as found, for instance, in the Book of Kells, but also the craft of the metalworker and enameller. The Ardagh and Derrynaflan chalices — some of Ireland's greatest religious treasures — almost certainly owe their existence to monastic workshops which were also involved in creating the reliquary shrines which are displayed so prominently in the National Museum in Dublin.

These monasteries had come into being during the sixth century in particular, and took on the task of providing religious services — the sacraments and burial, among others — for the laity living around about, much as parishes do today. In their first flush of religious fervour, they began to send out members of their community to spread knowledge of the gospels in places far away — a trend started by St Columba when he founded the monastery of Iona in the Outer Hebrides.

But laxity in the practice of monastic rules inevitably set in and, by the seventh and eighth centuries, it was largely only the ascetics — some of whom lived apart from the monastery — who were practising the true spirit of the religious life. The abbots tended to become secularised — many had families and probably regarded the abbacy as a handy way of earning a living — a state of affairs which they were happy to allow to continue for generations. Many of the monks were called *manaig*, which can be translated as 'monks', but these were — for all intents and purposes — laymen, usually married, who tilled the monastic fields and offered their first-born to the church.

Monasteries even went to war with one another, usually losing some of their community in the process. They battled to preserve their wealth and possessions, for the monasteries had become well endowed with land and valuables through bequests and patronage. They had thereby tended to become almost small towns, with *manaig*, crafts people and a mixum-gatherum of hangers-on inhabiting the land outside the inner sanctum of the monastery where the abbot would have lived close to the church. This inner area would have had an open space known as a *platea* around which were grouped the single church (for centuries made of wood before stone began to be more widely used around 800), the abbot's quarters, the monks' houses, domestic buildings such as the kitchen or communal refectory — and, in the course of time, stone crosses and a round tower.

Because it is virtually the only Irish monastery to
have been excavated in full, Nendrum, close to the sea
in County Down, helps us to flesh out some of the details
of layout given in descriptions of monasteries as found, for
instance, in Adamnan's *Life of St Columba*. Nendrum has
three roughly concentric walls, the innermost containing a
church and a round tower, as well as the monks' cemetery.
Outside these, the other two circular areas would have
contained the domestic quarters of the monks and the
manaig — creating between them quite a hive of activity,
both industrial and agricultural.

While some of the monasteries would have come
into existence through royal patronage, the majority
would have been founded by local families who would
have donated the land and whose members would have
occupied the main offices of abbot and prior for centuries.
They would have offered hospitality to the traveller and
given fosterage to children placed in their care.

Some monasteries would appear to have almost taken
over the mantle of a pagan sanctuary near-by, as seems to
have been the case at Armagh and Old Kilcullen, where
the Christian foundations were located literally only a
hilltop away from the neighbouring pre-Christian sites
of Navan Fort and Dún Ailinne respectively. The famous
double monastery at Kildare, where monks and nuns lived
side by side but presumably largely out of sight of one
another, was ruled by an abbess and her bishop (initially
St Brigid and Conlaed respectively), and kept a sacred
fire alight which is something that also smacks of a
pagan origin.

Other monasteries were sited on rivers, such as St
Mullins in County Carlow on the River Barrow, or on
islands in lakes. Two fine examples of the latter are

Devenish in Lower Lough Erne, Co. Fermanagh, and
Inishcealtra, Co. Clare, in Lough Derg on the Shannon,
both with their churches and their round towers, which
make them so conspicuous from a distance. But some of
the most important Irish monasteries developed along
main roads, including Glendalough, which adjoined an
important passage through the Wicklow Mountains, and
Clonmacnoise, Co. Offaly, where the *Eiscir Riada*, ancient
Ireland's main east-west thoroughfare, crossed the River
Shannon — the most important north-south traffic artery.
The respective cathedrals of these two sites are among the
largest pre-Norman churches in the country and, as we
know from literary sources, both monasteries contained
a number of houses in addition to other churches and
crosses. Both are also likely to have built special stone
shrines around the tombs of their respective founders,
SS Kieran and Kevin, which served to attract the pilgrims
who would help to enhance the economic stability of the
monastic institutions.

Kells in County Meath and Lusk in north Dublin have
both left traces of their circular surrounding wall in the
layout of the modern streets, but it is also remarkable how
once-important monasteries such as Clonard in County
Meath and Bangor on the shores of Belfast Lough have left
scarcely a trace of their former presence in the landscape.

Traces of monasteries' domestic buildings have
managed to survive in the western half of Ireland because
they were built of stone which, fortunately, was the
building material most easy to come by there. The
enclosure on the island of Inishmurray off the Sligo coast
comprises one or two huts or houses, as well as a church
and a saint's shrine, while the island of Skellig Michael off
the Kerry coast retains a number of well-preserved beehive

huts. It is only with difficulty that we could imagine such
stone huts to have been present in the richer monasteries
of the east and midlands of Ireland, where the monks'
domestic quarters are likely to have been made of wood
and, consequently, have not survived.

Inishmurray and Skellig Michael encapsulate more
the ascetic atmosphere of the early monasteries, whereas
the larger establishments such as Clonmacnoise, Kells and
Glendalough, show a more secular side which must
initially have looked very different to what we see
surviving today. The stone churches and crosses surviving
on the larger sites were not erected until about the third or
fourth century of the monastery's existence, and we tend
to forget that, during their formative period in the age of
the great founding saints, all of the buildings would have
been made of wood.

Devenish, Co. Fermanagh

Corbelled Huts and Oratories

The Dingle Peninsula, the most northerly of the five fingers which stretch out to welcome the Gulf Stream on the south-west coast of Ireland, is full of ancient field monuments — huts, oratories, churches, ogham stones, cross-decorated pillars, and many more — which present us with puzzles about their origin that are difficult to solve. One reason for this is that the historical sources are silent about them, though we do at least learn that the people who lived in the area during the medieval period were known as the Corca Dhuibhne, whose descendants cultivate that lovely brand of Irish which is still widely spoken there today. Another reason is that the nature of many of the monuments does not offer any obvious answer as to their use.

Take the beehive huts, for example. These are round stone structures built on the corbel principle, that is, constructed by layers of stones being laid in circles, one on top of the other, each getting narrower as they rise until the circle is closed by a single stone at the top, some 12–15 feet (4–5m) above the ground. When R. A. S. Macalister counted the number of these structures a century ago, he produced the surprising total of 414. He thought that they formed part of an intensive prehistoric settlement. Others have suggested that these beehive huts were erected by shepherds, who came here during the summer months as part of their transhumance way of life to provide seasonal feeding for their flocks, as they moved them around from place to place. But why then are such huts not also found on other parts of the transhumance trail outside the Dingle Peninsula? Perhaps the clue lies

in the location of the two main concentrations of beehive
huts. The first of these lies west of Ventry strand, above
the road on the way to Slea Head, where you have to
trespass to get to them — which is why the landowners
ask you to pay to visit them. The second cluster is spread
along the valleys of the Milltown and Feohanagh rivers
directly at the western foot of Mount Brandon which,
because it was the goal of medieval pilgrims, may suggest
an explanation for the beehive huts in connection with
pilgrimage activity in the peninsula.

Efforts have been made in recent years to revive the
pilgrimage to Mount Brandon, which is recorded as
having existed some hundreds of years ago. The Christian
pilgrim was probably the successor to those prehistoric
people who almost certainly foregathered on an annual
basis around the top of Mount Brandon to pay homage to
Lug, the good god of the pagan Celts, whose festival was
celebrated at the end of July — almost certainly the same
time of year as the Christian pilgrimage which succeeded
it. At some stage, perhaps around 800, the name of St
Brendan came to be associated with this magnetic
mountain and, ever since, the pilgrimage has come to be
associated with this famous saint whose legendary voyages
may even have extended as far as discovering the east coast
of North America.

The old Ordnance Survey maps of 150 years ago
record a Saint's Road which led to the top of Mount
Brandon. Our land-based civilisation would automatically
expect that this old pilgrims' road would have led to the
mountain summit from the landward side, that is, from
further east along the Dingle Peninsula. Exactly the
opposite, however, is the case. According to the map, the
road to the summit can be traced back to near Ventry

Harbour, which is some dozen miles (20km) further
south-west as the crow flies. This must surely mean that
the pilgrims can only have trodden the Saint's Road to
Mount Brandon from the west — where there is only
ocean. Of course, there is another way up Mount Brandon
from the landward side to the east, but it is not marked on
the map by a Saint's Road, so that we can probably
presume that the majority of pilgrims came from the west
along the road to the mountain — and that they can only
have done so by arriving on the peninsula by sea. If these
maritime pilgrims had to wait at the foot of the mountain
before the clouds cleared from what is well known as a
dangerous peak (there is a sheer drop of at least a thousand
feet on the eastern side), or if they had to wait for a
favourable wind to waft them away from their landing
place at Ventry beach after they had successfully climbed
the holy mountain, then they would have needed
somewhere to stay. So what better explanation is there for
the beehive huts than as pilgrim hostels placed near the
beach where boats would have arrived and departed, and
also at the foot of the mountain where the pilgrims could
await before the all clear was given to allow them to climb
the mountain in safety — in short, Ireland's earliest
surviving bed and breakfast establishments!

The corbel technique which is ideal, and was
doubtless developed, for round buildings, was also adapted
for rectangular oratories — of which the best known is
Gallarus Oratory, also on the Dingle Peninsula. The
danger in such an adaptation is that the corbelling of the
parabolic curve may collapse in the middle of the long
wall. This has happened with most of the examples which
are known along the west coast of Ireland as far north as
the island of Inisglora, off Mayo's Belmullet Peninsula, but

the superb quality of the masonry in Gallarus Oratory has
enabled it to avoid collapse — but for how long, as too
many children (and others!) climb up the sloping roof?

Skellig Michael is another example where the corbel
principle has withstood the dangers of collapse in its two
oratories of Gallarus type and its beehive huts (which have
an almost square interior). This island, too, was a well-
known place of pilgrimage down to the last century,
which might help to explain the presence of these
corbelled buildings there. Further support for the link
between beehive huts and pilgrimage recently came to
light with the discovery of what seems like an oratory of
Gallarus type on the summit of one of Ireland's most
famous places of pilgrimage — Croagh Patrick in County
Mayo. The roof had caved in on this structure, but it gave
a calibrated radiocarbon date most likely to lie somewhere
between A.D. 430 and 890. The period between these
dates may well also indicate the *floruit* of some of the
corbelled structures on the Dingle Peninsula and on
Skellig Michael. But, being a very timeless method of
construction, one must be careful about suggesting dates
for the corbel system as used particularly in the beehive
huts in the Dingle Peninsula — for at least one of them
is known to have been built in our own century.

Gallarus
Oratory,
Co. Kerry

Cross-decorated Stones

'This place did Ternoc son of Ciaran the Little bequeath under the protection of Peter the Apostle' is the approximate translation of an early Irish inscription carved on an upright stone at Kilnasaggart in County Armagh. The stone is decorated with crosses of various kinds and, as the Ternoc of the inscription may be identical with the person of the same name who is recorded as having died around 714–716, the Kilnasaggart stone may perhaps be the oldest identifiable cross-inscribed stone in Ireland — though, on the basis of the language used in the inscription, this is far from proven. The stone at Kilmalkedar, Co. Kerry, inscribed with the alphabet could, however, also be a claimant for the honour.

Another early example — and here again opinions differ as to how early — is a fine upright slab with pedimented top, and an interlaced cross on each face, which stands in the churchyard at Fahan Mura, Co. Donegal. On the north side there is an inscription, 'Glory and Honour to Father and Son and to Holy Spirit', written, unusually, in Greek, giving proof — if such were needed — that the Irish had a knowledge of this classical language.

At the opposite end of the country, at Tullylease in County Cork, there is a beautifully carved flat slab bearing an inscription, this time in Latin, requesting that whosoever reads it should say a prayer for Berechtuine. Sadly, we cannot positively identify the person mentioned, whose name is more likely to have been Anglo-Saxon than Irish. But accompanying the inscription is a finely incised cross standing on a base and with expanding

terminals, all decorated with interlace and fretwork motifs
— and finding its closest parallels in no less a codex than
the famous Book of Lindisfarne, now in the British
Library in London. While the book is normally ascribed
to the period around 700, the stone could, however, be a
century or more later.

The kind of cross represented at Tullylease has
expanding ends to the limbs, and crosses of a similar
variety are frequently found on slabs at Clonmacnoise,
Co. Offaly. In fact, Clonmacnoise has by far the largest
collection of these cross-decorated slabs anywhere in
Ireland, the number running to more than 500, though
the great majority are in a fragmentary state, which is
why only a selection of some of the best preserved are
displayed in the interpretative centre there. One of these
asks for a prayer for Tuathal Saer ('the wright') who
cannot be identified, but who probably lived around the
ninth century. A slightly more degenerate cross-slab does,
however, bear the name of one individual who can be
identified with virtual certainty — that of Odrán háu
Eolais — who was a scribe at Clonmacnoise before he
died in 994. It is from such an inscription as this that it
has been widely accepted that these stones were slabs
marking the graves of the individuals named on them —
but only very few can be equated with historically
known personages.

The Clonmacnoise stones show a rich variety of
cross-types, suggesting that a workshop was turning out
these slabs probably over a number of centuries — and
we know that, for a long time, burial at Clonmacnoise
was considered a consummation devoutly to be wished.
But while that monastery has by far the largest number
of high-quality cross-inscribed stones, there are many

interesting collections scattered throughout the country, though far fewer have inscriptions than those at Clonmacnoise. Not very far away is the old monastic site of Gallen, near Ferbane, which has a comparable selection and, further down the Shannon, the island of Inishcealtra also has a wide variety, while Glendalough in County Wicklow can also claim the same for itself.

By no means all of these stones are attached to such well-known sites, as many are found at places which have little or no history attached to them. Examples of these which may be cited include Church Island in Lough Currane, Co. Kerry, or the Dingle Peninsula, where some of the stones have been gathered for display at the heritage centre in Ballyferriter, or a lesser-known site at Toureen Peakaun in Tipperary's Glen of Aherlow.

Other counties, too, can boast of their collections of cross-decorated slabs and, to name just one, County Down houses some examples in the little museum at the old monastic site at Nendrum, and others at Saul, the place where St Patrick is said to have died.

Fahan Mura, Co. Donegal

High Crosses

The great stone crosses of Ireland are among the country's most important contributions to the art of medieval Europe, and they probably also represent the greatest collection of figure sculpture to survive from the period of Charlemagne and the sons who succeeded him as Holy Roman Emperor.

They have two particularly characteristic features: the presence of a circle or ring around the junction of shaft and arms, and the application of figure sculpture to the body of the cross, a feature rarely encountered outside Britain and Ireland. Ringed crosses are usually described as Celtic because it is in the insular countries where Celtic is still spoken today — Ireland, Scotland and Wales — that such crosses are found, though it was probably from England that the Irish learned the idea of erecting large 'biblical' crosses in stone. The purpose of the ring may have been at least two-fold. A brief look at most of the crosses will reveal that the arms are not straight-sided, but have a constriction almost halfway along their length. Because of this 'notch', there would have been an awful danger that the weighty ends of the stone arms might snap off if they were not supported by the ring. But, in addition to this purely structural function, there was probably also a symbolic purpose behind the ring which normally surrounds the figure of the crucified Christ. For early Christians, the Crucifixion was taken to be the most significant event in the whole history of the universe, and we may see the ring, therefore, as also serving the purpose of being a cosmic symbol — a duality of function and symbol which need not surprise us in the least.

The application of figure sculpture to the shaft and arms of the cross might also be seen as having had a dual function — ornamentation of the cross while at the same time acting as a Bible in stone for those who were probably unable to read the sacred scriptures themselves. The figured panels illustrate scenes from both the Old and the New Testaments, as well as introducing us to the desert hermits Paul and Anthony who, as being in a sense the founders of monasticism in the Egyptian desert, could have been taken as the models and prototypes of Irish monks — and it may be said that the crosses are always found on old Irish monastic sites.

There is a wide choice of scriptural scenes on the crosses. From the Old Testament we are frequently presented with *Adam and Eve*, whose original sin was the first link in a chain of events which finally led to Christ giving his life for mankind on the cross. Their son *Cain* slaying their other child *Abel* — the first innocent victim of the Old Testament prefiguring Christ as the innocent victim of the New Testament — can be seen on Muiredach's Cross at Monasterboice, Co. Louth. Other scenes, found for instance on the cross at Moone, Co. Kildare, show how God saved the good in their time of peril: *Isaac* about to be sacrificed by his father *Abraham*; *Daniel* saved from death in the jaws of hungry lions, or the angel saving the *Three Hebrews* from being burned in a fiery furnace. The same theme of the help of God is continued for the New Testament at Moone, where we see the *Flight into Egypt* (an event which followed the Holy Family being warned of impending danger by the Lord's angel) and the *Multiplication of the Loaves and Fishes* (illustrating how those faithful to the Lord were saved from hungering by Christ's miracle on the Mount).

The choice of New Testament scenes reflects various
picture cycles associated with the life of Christ — his
childhood, his public life and his passion, death and
resurrection. Some crosses would seem to have had their
scenes chosen to illustrate a particular aspect of religious
dogma. The Cross of Muiredach at Monasterboice, for
instance, would seem to have Christ, Lord of the Earth
and Heavens, as its theme, while the Broken Cross at Kells,
Co. Meath, demonstrates the importance of the sacrament
of baptism by choosing a majority of scenes featuring the
beneficial power of water, including the *Baptism of Christ*.

Other crosses would seem to give the appearance of
a film strip, with their panels of biblical scenes shown one
after the other and arranged in the correct biblical order.
This is particularly the case in Northern Ireland where
crosses such as those at Arboe and Donaghmore, both in
Tyrone, demonstrate a fairly rigid separation of Old and
New Testaments which is not adhered to quite so strictly
in areas further south. The Tall or West Cross at
Monasterboice is one of the most noticeable examples
where the correct biblical order is not followed in the
arrangement of the events portrayed, suggesting that there
was some reason — no longer known to us — why the
scenes were grouped in a particular sequence. Because
such deep thought obviously went into the choice of
biblical themes, we can at least be sure that the rejection
of the biblical order was intentional. Understandably,
the closing events in Christ's life feature prominently,
and nowhere more obviously than on the Cross of the
Scriptures at Clonmacnoise, which places a very strong
emphasis on the passion, death and resurrection of Christ.
The Last Judgment is shown back to back with the
Crucifixion on this cross, as on so many others too.

There are probably about 85 crosses which bear some figure sculpture, but there are others where the cross itself (as opposed to the base) is purely decorative, being delicately engraved with geometrical ornament, as is the case at Ahenny, Co. Tipperary.

The dating of all of these crosses is currently the subject of much discussion, but it ought to be pointed out that, in general, there are two main chronological groups of crosses, widely separated in time. The earlier of the two can be said to concentrate around the later ninth century, though some within this group are probably earlier and others later. It is only recently that it has become apparent that inscriptions indicate that one cross — at Castlebernard, Co. Offaly — was erected at the behest of the High King, Maelsechlainn I, between 846 and 862, and another — the Cross of the Scriptures at Clonmacnoise — erected by his son some decades later. We cannot identify the Muiredeach who is mentioned in the inscription on the cross which he had erected at Monasterboice, and we are left even more to guess the date of those crosses which bear no inscriptions at all. We are equally in the dark about why crosses were erected. Here, too, there may be a number of possibilities — as a poor man's Bible in stone, to demarcate boundaries rather than marking burials (which they apparently did not, unlike their modern counterparts), to induce feelings of piety in those visiting the monastery or, quite simply, just to impress.

The crosses of the earlier grouping are largely found — for whatever reason — in the provinces of Leinster and Ulster, with concentrations in the midlands and east Meath, the Barrow Valley and the region in the north around Armagh. In contrast, the later group of crosses,

almost all assignable to the twelfth century, are found in
the provinces of Munster and Connacht from whence
most of the high kings of the period came, showing
clearly the importance of political patronage in the
erection of the crosses. These later crosses usually have
only very few biblical scenes, though *Adam and Eve* make
their appearance more than once. Even the *Crucifixion*
becomes a rarity. Instead, the figure of the benevolent and
triumphant Christ stands out in high relief on the head
of the cross, the only other major figure being a bishop
or abbot connected with the monastery on which the
cross stands. Good examples are found on the Rock of
Cashel and Roscrea, both in County Tipperary, Dysert
O'Dea, Co. Clare, Tuam, Co. Galway, and Glendalough,
Co. Wicklow.

After 1200, the high crosses seem to go out of
fashion, though the ringed form was revived in the mid-
nineteenth century as a symbol of the nationalist revival,
but these modern copies acting as gravestones can rarely
be compared in quality with the originals which they
nearly suffocate, as demonstrated so well in the case of
Muiredach's Cross at Monasterboice.

Adam and Eve, Broken Cross, Kells, Co. Meath

Round Towers

When the Irish people wanted to build a monument to their great liberator, Daniel O'Connell, the man who had led the country out of the dark bondage of the penal days into the light of Catholic emancipation, they erected a round tower over his grave in Glasnevin Cemetery. It was an appropriate choice of monument, as round towers ranked on a par with shamrock, harps, the Celtic cross and the Irish wolfhound as the powerful symbols of the rising swell of Irish nationalist pride emerging in the middle of the last century. This was not without reason, let it be said, for the country had a virtual monopoly of these monuments so redolent of the Golden Age of Ireland's great monasteries. Scotland has two such towers, and the Isle of Man one, whereas Ireland can proudly boast of 65 examples, spread over almost every single one of the island's thirty-two counties.

Some are, of course, better preserved than others, but the most complete — such as those in Antrim, Co. Antrim, Clondalkin, Co. Dublin, or Killala, Co. Mayo — rise to a height of up to 100 feet (30m) at the top where they narrow into a neat conical cap. That at Glendalough, Co. Wicklow, has such a delicate taper — said to be 1 in 77 — that it almost resembles a well-pared pencil standing on its end, but the proportions of others are rather plumper, and all bear testimony to the skill of the old Irish master-masons in constructing tall buildings.

Inside there were up to seven individual floor landings, lit by small windows and linked by steep wooden stairs — none of which has survived — but towers at Devenish, Co. Fermanagh, Kildare and Kilkenny are among those where modern replacements have been inserted to allow the visitor to climb to the top and enjoy the splendid panorama from the four top windows. One curious feature is the placing of the doorway usually at a height of about 10–12 feet (4m) above the base — the tower on Scattery Island in the Shannon estuary being an exception, in having the entrance at ground level.

Despite all their prominence which adds a welcome vertical presence to the undulating horizontals in the Irish landscape, we know surprisingly little about these towers. More than a century and a half ago, the dilettanti thought they were built by the Vikings or the Phoenicians, and to serve as hermits' pillar perches, fire temples or even phallic symbols. George Petrie who earned his title of Father of Irish Archaeology through an essay on these towers published in 1845 was, however, the first to point out that they should all be understood in a purely Christian context, and rightly so, as they are all associated with early Irish monasteries, of which they sometimes remain the only visible trace.

By equating these towers with what the old Irish historical sources described as a *cloigthech*, or literally 'bell-house', Petrie described them as belfries, making them therefore into Ireland's answer to the Italian campanile or the Islamic minaret. The Irish may indeed have got the idea for these towers from Mediterranean lands, though Italy's best-known campanile, the Leaning Tower of Pisa, is centuries younger than its nearest Irish counterpart at Kilmacduagh, Co. Galway, where the tower leans two feet out of plumb at the top! By combing through old Irish historical annals, Petrie was also able to state that the towers served to protect people and store treasures in times of trouble.

That trouble was considered to have been caused by
the nasty Viking hordes descending upon the old Irish
monasteries in order to carry off the church valuables back
home with them to Scandinavia. But, in the meantime,
we have now to face the reality that it was just as much
the nasty Irish who did the raiding, and that the earliest
recorded towers were built after the worst of the Viking
onslaughts had passed. The Irish annals record the
existence of some 23 such towers between 948 and 1238,
but only in the rarest instance are we told when a tower
was built, as opposed to when it was damaged or
destroyed. Indeed, it is often very difficult to date any
single tower unless it bears decoration on the doorway
or elsewhere in the ornamental Romanesque style of the
twelfth century, as is the case at Devenish, Co. Fermanagh,
or Timahoe, Co. Laois — and to this period the graceful
example at Ardmore, Co. Waterford, may also be ascribed.

The raising of the doorway well above ground level
has led to the widespread belief that the towers were
essentially defensive. It was thought that the monks would
have had a movable ladder which they would have pulled
up after them before closing the door on the adversaries
from whom they were trying to escape, and would then
have run up to the top from where they would have pelted
their enemies with stones. But the defence theory loses
weight when it is considered how easy it would have been
to fire a flaming arrow in through one of the windows
after which the draught from below would have quickly
turned the wooden stairs and landings into a blazing
inferno, as was probably the case when the tower at
Monasterboice, Co. Louth, went up in flames in the year
1097 along with its many books and treasures. But this
leaves us no nearer a solution to the question of why

the doorways were located so high above the ground —
one of the great enigmas of these towers.

Nor is it altogether clear why the towers were so high.
Did belfries have to be so tall that the sound of the bell
could be heard far and wide? Or was their height designed
to direct the monks' minds towards celestial thoughts
about how best to get a high place in heaven? Or could it
have been that the towers acted as a kind of beacon to
show foot-weary pilgrims where their goal lay, and to give
them encouragement to complete the last few miles of
their long journey? Certainly, the first inkling the modern
traveller gets of his or her approach to Clonmacnoise or
Glendalough is the upper part of a round tower peering
up over a low ridge or rising above surrounding trees as if
it were a rocket about to take off from Cape Canaveral.

Like many things in Ireland, there is probably no one
simple or single explanation for the presence and purpose
of round towers. As George Petrie discovered, they may
have served to protect people and monastic treasures, but
they could have functioned as a kind of 'lighthouse' for
approaching pilgrims and other travellers, and they may
also have been belfries. Or were they? The Dutch scholar
A. N. Koldeweij has recently suggested that the old Irish
word for these towers, *cloigthech* or 'bell-house', should
be taken, not in the sense of a belfry, but as a house where
bells were kept before being taken home as souvenirs by
pilgrims who came to venerate relics on the site. But that
would still not explain why the doors were so high
above ground!

Romanesque Churches

'Small is beautiful' is a phrase which can be applied to the Romanesque churches of Ireland — those which use the round arch in their doorways, arches and windows, much as the ancient Romans did. Certainly, in comparison with their English and continental counterparts — Durham, Speyer, Vézelay or Santiago de Compostela — they are small in scale, but they are also very attractive because of the beautiful carving which twelfth-century stonemasons contributed to their embellishment.

Developed in eleventh-century France, Romanesque as a style of architecture and decoration did not reach Ireland until the second quarter of the twelfth century, by which time the style which was to succeed it — the pointed-arched Gothic — had already begun to develop in England and France. The introduction of Romanesque into Ireland can be linked closely with the religious reform movement which emanated from England and took root in the southern half of Ireland after an important synod at Cashel in 1101, when the Rock of Cashel was handed over to the Church. It is no surprise, therefore, that the architectural style caught on initially in the province of Munster where the reform movement was strongest, and that its first great exponent was perched in a prominent position on top of that very rock. This is the building known as Cormac's Chapel erected, we presume, between 1127 and 1134, and including so many novelties in its design that it must have struck awe into its contemporary beholders. Virtually all preceding stone churches in Ireland had the sole entrance in the west wall. Not so Cormac's

Chapel, which had the main doorway unusually in the
north wall, as well as two others in addition. Another
innovation was the placing of tall towers where transepts
would stand in modern churches and, on the south side, a
series of blind arcades raised one above the other on the
outside wall. Its crowning glory was a stone roof, a feature
imitated in St Flannan's Church at Killaloe and St Kevin's
in Glendalough, among others. Thus, Cormac's Chapel
became a model to be copied — not *in toto,* for the sum
of its innovations was too much to be incorporated into
any one other single building — but at least in individual
details. Near the western end of Munster, in County
Kerry, the blind arcading was imitated at Kilmalkedar
and in St Brendan's Cathedral, Ardfert, but also somewhat
closer to Cashel, on the façade of St Cronan's Church
at Roscrea.

Another Kerry church helps us with a much-needed
chronological 'anchor' which is sadly lacking for almost
all other Irish Romanesque churches. This is Aghadoe,
with its incomparable panorama over the lakes of
Killarney, and in the *Annals* written on one of their
islands, Inisfallen — itself the home of yet another scenic
Romanesque church — we learn that a storm in 1282
broke down the 'great church of Achad Deó' which had
been standing undamaged for six score years and four, thus
giving us a date of 1158. For some others, however, we
can get an idea of the period of construction through
historically recognisable personalities who were probably
associated with them. As an example, the Nuns' Church
at Clonmacnoise was built, it is said, by Dervorgilla, the
lady who unwittingly and indirectly brought about the
Norman invasion through being abducted by Diarmait
MacMurrough who, himself, probably had his name

inscribed on the colourful doorway at Killeshin in County Laois. Numerous other Romanesque churches fill out our picture of the twelfth century, and the style of carving survived into the first quarter of the following century in areas west of the Shannon.

It is particularly on the doorways and on the arches between the larger nave and smaller chancel that most of the Romanesque decoration is to be found lavished. Very common is the chevron or zig-zag ornament which was probably copied from English churches of the period — even before the Norman invasion. Foliate scrolls and animal interlace (ultimately of Viking origin) can also be found, but rather rarer are the human heads (often with high cheek-bones and ears) as found in the remarkable reassembled doorway at Dysert O'Dea in County Clare. Though probably made up of stones derived from two totally different doorways, this portal shows a very wide variety of motifs current in Irish Romanesque carving in the west of Ireland. The Church of Ireland Cathedral at Kilmore in County Cavan is another fine example of the reuse and reassemblage of Romanesque carved stones in a secondary position.

A further cathedral with a collection of reassembled Romanesque sculpture is Ardmore in County Waterford, where *Adam and Eve* and the *Judgment of Solomon* make their appearance among carved stones inserted into the west wall of the edifice. Adam and Eve recur in carvings in the Romanesque church at Kilteel in County Kildare, but other twelfth-century architectural sculpture frequently concentrates on the *Crucifixion* and *Passion of Christ*, as on the lintels at Maghera, Co. Derry, and Raphoe, Co. Donegal. The subject matter of some small figure sculptures of the Romanesque period, as at

Freshford, Co. Kilkenny, or Tuam, Co. Galway, cannot
be identified, but the more ornamental rather than figure
sculpture of the Romanesque in Ireland was probably
symbolic — but of what we do not know. It is difficult to
probe the minds of the sculptors who created the weird
and wonderful carvings of Irish Romanesque and, rather
than attempting to do so, it is preferable to concentrate on
admiring the skill and artistry with which they have
adorned these small and wonderful churches.

The mason–sculptors frequently used sandstone, as it
was an easy material to handle, but it has also tended to
lose the sharpness of its detail down the centuries, as is
sadly the case with that great apogee of Irish Romanesque
— the doorway of Clonfert Cathedral in County Galway.
More protected from the elements down the years, the
Romanesque decoration of the chancel arch of Tuam
Cathedral and the doorway inserted at the western end of
Killaloe Cathedral are, however, much better preserved.
Together with the chancel arch of the hauntingly beautiful
church at Monaincha, Co. Tipperary, they give us an idea
of how splendid and how crisp the carving must have been
when first created some seven hundred years ago.

Nuns' Church, Clonmacnoise, Co. Offaly

Cistercian Abbeys

The introduction of the Cistercians into Ireland reads almost like a fairytale. When St Malachy of Armagh, the great twelfth-century reformer, was on his way to Rome in 1140, he stopped off at Clairvaux and struck up an immediate friendship there with the abbot, St Bernard, to such an extent that he subsequently requested the Pope to allow him to spend the rest of his life in the French monastery. But it must have been the Holy Spirit which directed the Pope to tell St Malachy that he should return to his native country — for Ireland needed his reforming spirit more than Clairvaux did. Nevertheless, within two years Malachy brought over some of St Bernard's French monks to found the first Irish Cistercian house at Mellifont in County Louth. They added new life to the Church reform movement which had been gathering momentum since the beginning of the twelfth century, even if this went hand in hand with the almost terminal decline of many of the old Irish monasteries (some of which, however, managed to cling on to life for a few centuries more).

In comparison with the somewhat loose layout of these older Irish monasteries, the Cistercians were — as far as we know — the first to introduce the new continental monastic ground plan into Ireland. This was based on a grassy area known as a cloister garth, around which there was a cloister, usually covered over with a lean-to roof. At one end of this usually rectangular garth lay the church, with nave and transepts, and with a chancel which was frequently vaulted in stone — very much the exception rather than the rule in medieval Ireland. Where the

transepts met with the long east/west axis of the church,
a tower was usually added later — a dominant, if chubby
and squat addition to the monastic skyline. At right angles
to the church, one longer side of the cloister gave access to
the sacristy, the chapter house (where the monks listened
to Bible readings and conducted the business of the day)
and the abbot's quarters, as well as a narrow passage,
known as a slype, which led outside to the monks' burial
ground. Opposite the church side of the garth lay the
kitchen and the refectory. In front of the Mellifont
refectory there is a beautiful octagonal two-storey lavabo,
where the monks could wash their hands before and after
meals, and beside it a portion of the original cloister has
been reconstructed. The fourth side was given over to the
storehouse and, on the upper floor, the communal
dormitory from which the monks could descend to the
church via special stairs to say the divine office in the
middle of the night. Theirs was not an easy life. They did
not become monks to enjoy themselves, but rather to offer
their lives to God, and their works included much physical
labour in the fields, for they were among the first in
Ireland to have organised agriculture on a large scale.

Between the initiation of Mellifont in 1142 and their
last monastic foundation at Hore Abbey, near Cashel, one
hundred and thirty years later, the Cistercians managed to
found a total of 36 houses in Ireland, and these are among
the most fascinating monastic buildings ever constructed
in the country. One building which spans a good deal of
this period is Boyle Abbey in County Roscommon, where
we can see many phases of activity between the start,
around 1160, and the period of its completion, around
1220. Its earliest portion, the chancel, was started in the
round-arched Romanesque style, but the north arcade of

the nave is constructed in the pointed Gothic style
which the Cistercians helped to popularise in Ireland.
The capitals, particularly of the nave, are carved with
interesting animals and human figures of a kind heartily
disapproved of by St Bernard.

Boyle was only one of a number of Irish Cistercian
monasteries colonised from Mellifont. Another daughter
house was Baltinglass, on the River Slaney in County
Wicklow, which was founded in 1148 by Diarmait
MacMurrough, the man responsible for having introduced
the Normans into Ireland. There the stout round and
square supports of the nave arcade contain interesting
geometrical carvings which are further echoed in another
famous Cistercian house further to the south — at
Jerpoint in the County of Kilkenny. But Jerpoint's most
famous sculptures are those on the cloister arcade, added
during the first half of the fifteenth century and containing
figures of saints, knights and their ladies, as well as a small
menagerie of indefinable animals.

Because they were nearly always located out in the
countryside, the Cistercian abbeys still enjoy attractive
settings undisturbed by modern developments, as in the
case of the two Ulster houses of Inch and Grey Abbey,
Co. Down, though a small town has grown up close to
the latter. But even more splendid in its isolation is
Corcomroe, located near the northern end of the stony
wastes of the Burren in County Clare. Among the
limestone crags grows a rich variety of plants which
helped to give the monastery its cognomen, St Mary of
the Fertile Rock. This is reflected in the naturalistic
carvings on some of the capitals which represent unusual
species like the opium poppy, and possibly deadly
nightshade and lily-of-the-valley, which the monks may

have copied from what they had planted in their herb
garden or from drawings in a herbal manuscript.

In addition to the various houses founded from
Mellifont, there were others which were founded after
the invasion by the Normans — and with their assistance
— such as Dunbrody in Wexford. With time, the Norman
foundations gained in power and were opposed to the
Irish-dominated monasteries, leading to the famous
Conspiracy of Mellifont in 1227/8 when the Irish monks
refused to co-operate with an English monk sent to
inspect them, whereupon the Irish abbots were deposed
— but things were later patched up between the two
sides, at least to some extent.

The Irish Cistercians had started a number of their
churches before the arrival of the Normans but, together
with them, they were the great church builders of the
twelfth and thirteenth centuries in Ireland. It is their
foundation at Graiguenamanagh which gives us the best
impression of the majestic simplicity of one of their early
Irish churches. It has little architectural sculpture —
conforming to the precepts of St Bernard — but the
mouldings and vaulted arches of stone (in so far as they
survive) create a decorative pattern against the overall
whitewashing of the walls. Graiguenamanagh succeeds in
impressing its beauty upon us because it was restored in
the best of taste and with a great deal of local effort, pride
and enthusiasm, in the years leading up to 1980. Its
cloister buildings still lie hidden beneath a Victorian
overlay, but it is to be hoped that one day they will rise
like the phoenix to make the whole ensemble one of the
great Cistercian complexes of medieval Ireland, outclassing
what was, in fact, the largest and presumably the most
opulent of all Irish Cistercian houses — that of St Mary's

in Dublin, of which only the chapter house survives.
Its foundations may, however, with luck be excavated
some day, as they too lie beneath a much later covering
of buildings.

    During the later Middle Ages, the Cistercians
confined themselves largely to restoring their older
foundations, rather than opening new houses. Of the
few abbeys which did, however, undergo a considerable
rebuild during this period, the best known is undoubtedly
Holy Cross in County Tipperary, and it has been once
more restored to its former glory during the third quarter
of our own century, so that its fine vaulting and decorative
stonework — perhaps the finest of the Irish later Middle
Ages — could be shown off to best advantage. By an Act
of Parliament in 1969, the state handed over the buildings
to the Catholic Church and assisted in its restoration,
which culminated in a rededication ceremony in 1975.
Like Graiguenamanagh, it is a wonderful testimony to
Cistercian construction brought to life once again through
local vision and tenacity, and presented to the public for
all to see now and enjoy.

Boyle Abbey, Co. Roscommon

Medieval Cathedrals

After the medieval Church in Ireland had set up dioceses and bishoprics in the twelfth century, its first cathedrals were built in the round-arched Romanesque style — but only parts of these remain, as at Ardfert in County Kerry, where the arcades in the west wall survived by being incorporated into the design of the later Gothic cathedral. Another cathedral associated with St Brendan, at Clonfert, Co. Galway, has the most elaborate Romanesque portal in the country, also leading into what is largely a Gothic structure.

Where expanding congregations required it, bishops were prepared to demolish a whole Romanesque cathedral to make way for a thirteenth-century successor, as was the case at St Canice's Cathedral, Kilkenny. But they were also prepared to change their building style in the course of construction to keep up with the latest fashion, and this we can see most clearly in Christ Church Cathedral in Dublin where transepts and, we presume, the original choir were built in a late Romanesque style around the 1180s and 1190s. But, within a few decades, the adjoining nave had been completed in the contrasting Gothic style, constructed by masons from the west of England — though there may have been a gap of some years between the two sections. Christ Church was full of innovations in an Irish context — a crypt running the full length of the structure, the peculiar late Romanesque undercut chevron ornament of doorways and windows which was later to find its way to the west of Ireland, and the three superimposed levels in the elevation of the Gothic nave. But the collapse of the nave vault in 1562, which also brought down the whole of the south wall with it, was the beginning of a disastrous decline in the state of the edifice that was not halted until the 1870s when the fabric was thoroughly restored by the eminent Victorian architect, George Edmund Street.

While he was fitfully occupied in Dublin, Street was also supervising the large-scale reconstruction of another important Irish Gothic cathedral — that of St Brigid at Kildare, which had been started by Bishop Ralph of Bristol in 1223. When Street surveyed the cathedral ruins, the west wall had long disappeared, the tower had been half blasted away by cannon fire in 1641, and the only operational part of the structure was the choir which had been a seventeenth-century reconstruction. Only the south transept, the side walls of the nave and the south wall of the tower were retained from the original building, but without Street's work and the initiative of local fundraisers which made it possible, Kildare Cathedral would not have become the noble house of God which it is today.

We must return to Dublin for yet a third Gothic cathedral which underwent considerable restoration in the nineteenth century, and this is St Patrick's, which stands only a few hundred yards from Christ Church but, unlike it, lay outside the old town walls. Whereas Christ Church had been restored by Henry Roe, a whiskey distiller, it was the Irishman's love of a pint which enabled Sir Benjamin Lee Guinness to pay for the reconstruction of St Patrick's. It is more uniform in its architecture than Christ Church, using throughout the Early English style of the first half of the thirteenth century, and it was probably completed by 1254.

An approximate contemporary is St Canice's
Cathedral in Kilkenny which, unlike its Dublin
counterparts, had a wooden ceiling which reduced the
weight on the walls and allowed them to be interspersed
with more windows, thus giving the interior — and
particularly that of the choir — a luminous quality all of
its own. Restored more in detail than in substance in the
last century, St Canice's stands as one of the most
genuinely well preserved of all Ireland's medieval
cathedrals, but it should also share that claim with St
Flannan's Cathedral at Killaloe, which likewise retains
much of its thirteenth-century fabric. Both of these in
their own way can be proud of their architectural
decoration — heads in the case of Kilkenny, and undercut
chevron decoration of the windows at Killaloe.

The North of Ireland has also been assiduous in
preserving what it can of its Gothic cathedrals, and these
again belong to the great cathedral-building age of the
thirteenth century. Armagh — burial place of Brian Boru
— was, however, largely restored in the nineteenth
century, but in Downpatrick a considerable amount of the
original stonework is preserved, and its seemingly smaller
scale gives it a more homely appearance inside. A third
example, St Columb's in the city of Derry, is Gothic in
style but not really medieval, as it was built between 1628
and 1633 in imitation of large English medieval parish
churches to serve as a place of divine worship for the
newly established planters who had come from England
and Scotland within the previous decade and a half.

Coming away further south again, there are other
examples still in use which are sometimes unjustly
neglected — Lismore, Cloyne, Ferns and Leighlin.
These cathedrals may not be of great architectural

importance, but they do help to preserve the unbroken link with medieval Ireland. The same, of course, can also be said of St Mary's Cathedral in Limerick which, from Romanesque beginnings, developed into a Gothic cathedral bearing some of the hallmarks of Cistercian architecture. It is noteworthy not only for having had a number of side chapels added to it during the later Middle Ages but also for its wonderfully carved wooden choirstalls or misericords, unique in Ireland.

Not far to the north is one of the smallest and poorest of the Irish medieval cathedrals — that at Kilfenora in the Burren. Its nave is still used for divine service by the Church of Ireland, which is the institution that took over these charming old medieval cathedrals of Ireland and managed to preserve them for us down to our own day — something for which we should be eternally grateful. What could have happened if the Church of Ireland had not taken on this onerous and costly task is seen in the chancel of Kilfenora Cathedral, which has lost its roof (though maintaining many interesting monuments within). But proof of the point can also be found in much more inspiring piles — the cathedrals at Ardfert, Co. Kerry, Ardmore, Co. Waterford, and — one of the noblest of them all — the cathedral on the Rock of Cashel, set on fire around 1485, it is said, because the Earl of Kildare thought the archbishop was inside.

Norman Castles

For the ancient Irish, warring was partially something of a summer pastime: I raid your cattle this year, and you come with a small warlike band to reclaim them — and a few more — next year, type of thing. But the style of warfare changed utterly after the Normans landed on the Wexford coast in 1169. It was not just livestock the new invading barons were interested in grabbing, it was the grazing land too. What they won by the sword they determined to keep, and entrenched themselves to ensure that the Irish would not take it back from them.

In establishing their hegemony, they started erecting large flat-topped mounds, known as mottes, with a wooden tower on top. Not a single one of these towers has managed to survive the Irish weather down the centuries, but the later medieval stone tower atop the motte at Clough in County Down gives us an inkling of what the combination would have looked like when silhouetted against the skyline.

The Normans built their earthworks not only upwards, but outwards as well, creating a ring-work or circular wall with a gatehouse which, in essence, was not greatly different from the native Irish rath or ring-fort. Within less than a decade of their arrival, the Normans had, in addition, started to build stone castles. One, built on top of just such a ring-work, was the most extensive Norman castle ever constructed in Ireland, namely Trim Castle in County Meath. In the middle of an extensive D-shaped area, defended by a stout curtain wall and a moat once filled with water from the Boyne, stands a tall, square tower with a smaller tower projecting from each

side, which may have been erected as much to impress
as to defend.

Even better preserved, however, is the other great
early Norman castle which, this time, stands on a rock
jutting out into Belfast Lough at Carrickfergus,
Co. Antrim. Put up by John de Courcy to consolidate
his Ulster gains shortly after he had marched into the
province in 1177, the massive tower or donjon had
accommodation for the victorious baron on the top floor,
and for his staff and guards down below. From his vantage
point he could look down on an extensive hall close by,
where the garrison would have foregathered.

Such halls were a more common feature within
the castle walls than was hitherto suspected, as recent
excavations at Trim and Limerick have revealed. At Adare,
in County Limerick, there are two such halls beside the
thirteenth-century castle, and Newcastle West, not far
away, has also been found to have one of the same date.
Adare used a river to defend the castle on one side, as did
that which King John had built on the banks of the
Shannon at Limerick around 1200, and water was also
used as an added defence at Trim and Carrickfergus.
When we visit what is probably the longest utilised of all
Norman castles in Ireland, namely Dublin Castle itself,
we often fail to realise today that it, too, was formerly
surrounded by water, some of it provided by the (now
underground) River Poddle flowing into a pool on the
south side of the castle — that famous dark pool, the
Dubh Linn in Irish, which gives the city its modern name.

Some of the most dramatically sited of all Norman
defences in Ireland are, not surprisingly, those on top of
rocks. One example which might not readily spring to
mind is Roche's Castle in County Louth, guarding an

important passage to and from the north. Though its interior is not particularly exciting, its drama is best appreciated from below, where its extensive wall seems virtually impregnable on the edge of a steep cliff. Much the same applies to the rather damaged remains of Dunamase Castle in County Laois, with a silhouette which can clearly be made out from the Cork to Dublin road not far from Portlaoise.

Castleknock on the outskirts of Dublin had another fine example of a Norman castle on a rock, but its condition has sadly deteriorated since it was first sketched by an artist named Francis Place in 1698. Somewhat better preserved is Carlingford Castle, perched on a rock overlooking the inlet of Carlingford Lough, where King John may have been attracted by the taste of its still-famous oysters. Carrigogunnell, not far from the southern shore of the Shannon estuary, was in a position to monitor shipping plying to and from the city of Limerick, but surely the most magnificently sited seaside Norman-style castle in Ireland is Dunluce in County Antrim. There, however, only a small portion could possibly be attributed to the Norman period — the remainder belongs to the sixteenth and seventeenth centuries, abandoned when a part of it slid into the foamy brine, bringing many of the servants with it to a watery grave.

Where the Normans felt the necessity to entrench themselves on flatter ground, they frequently built a castle which was square or roughly rectangular in shape, with rounded turrets at each corner, and often with twin drum-towers protecting the entrance in the middle of one side. Ballymote in Sligo was square in shape, and Roscommon Castle in the neighbouring county was closer to a rectangle, its form perhaps inspiring the O'Conor kings

of Connacht to imitate it at Ballintubber. The Leinster
castles in Carlow town and at Ferns in County Wexford
share a similar ground-plan — but also a similar ruinous
condition, the former having been blown up in 1814 by
a doctor who was trying to convert it into a lunatic
asylum! But while also much altered down the centuries,
Kilkenny Castle gives us perhaps the best idea of what
one of these Norman castles with massive round corner
turrets looked like.

Nenagh Castle in County Tipperary had one of
its towers round and rising to a height of about 60 feet
(18m), while Dundrum, Co. Down, and Shanid, Co.
Limerick, had totally free-standing rounded donjons or
towers rising high within the castle walls. Not even the
many layers of later wrapping around Athlone Castle can
conceal the unusual ten-sided shape of the once free-
standing tower which guarded the important Shannon
crossing, made famous by the siege of 1691.

Two Norman towers may finally be mentioned as
they look towards the later development of the tower-
houses — Athenry Castle of 1238, and the gateway to
Roscrea Castle built about forty years later, both of
which are well preserved.

While some of the great Norman castles in Ireland,
most notably Trim and Carrickfergus, can clearly be dated
to the twelfth century, it was the period 1200 to 1300
which saw the building of the majority of Norman castles.
The devastation associated with the presence in Ireland of
the Bruce brothers from Scotland during the years 1315
to 1318 marked the first notable decline of Norman castle
construction in Ireland, but it was the totally debilitating
bubonic plague known as the Black Death of 1347–50
which finally brought it to an abrupt end.

Medieval Walled Towns

Walls, as we have already seen, surrounded early medieval monasteries, but it was the Vikings who introduced the first purely secular towns — and town walls — to Ireland. Prime among these was Dublin, where the Norsemen established themselves along the Liffey banks around 841. Within a century they had constructed a wall made of earth, and it may have had a palisade of wood on top of it to add further protection. Waterford, another town founded by the Vikings, was enclosed by an earthen defence in the eleventh century. Of these earthen banks little is now to be seen and, instead, it is the stone walls which have left their most visible mark among the defended medieval towns of Ireland.

As the capital city and centre of power, Dublin naturally had its own set of stone walls, but the vicissitudes of history have left it with only a few stretches — most notably along Cook Street, parallel to the Liffey. One of the rounded towers along its length, Isolde's Tower on Lower Exchange Street/Essex Quay was, however, excavated recently at a depth considerably below street level, and it proved to have high-quality ashlar masonry in its construction. Waterford, however, has fared somewhat better in having longer stretches of wall, as well as towers, preserved along its length. These towers, which protruded out from the wall, were designed to give a better firing range against those trying to undermine the wall than could be provided by archers or, later, musketeers, standing on the parapets on top of the long straight stretches of wall. Waterford, too, has what may be considered the strongest tower in any Irish town wall, that known as Reginald's Tower, located at a prominent corner of the town near where the small St John's river flows into the River Suir. Often taken to be part of the original Viking defences of the city, it was probably given its present form by the Normans during the thirteenth century.

Vying with it in significance is St Laurence's Gate in Drogheda, which is of roughly the same period. Drogheda was unusual, though not unique, among Irish medieval towns in that it was fortified on both sides of the river which bisected it. St Laurence's Gate controlled the entrance from the sea in the northern half of the town. It is not so much a gate as a double-tower known as a barbican which stood outside the gate to act as an added protection for the entrance which, of course, was where any town was weakest. Gates not only controlled access and egress, they were also the most suitable locations to collect tolls on merchandise being brought in and out of the town.

Some actual town gates have come down to us in a fairly intact condition from the Middle Ages. The County Limerick town of Kilmallock has two — 'King's Castle' and 'Blossom's Gate' — each on a main road radiating from the town centre. The town of Athenry in County Galway is another good example where a town gate has been well preserved, and it is further distinguished by having what is perhaps the longest single stretch of medieval town wall anywhere in the country. Some of it at least was probably built by the De Burgo and De Bermingham victors of a battle in 1316 against the Irish king Felim O'Conor and his supporters of Edward Bruce, whose arms and armour were sold to pay for constructing the town walls.

Further medieval examples deserve at least brief
mention here. Youghal has a long stretch of town wall
above St Mary's Protestant parish church which, while
heavily restored, gives the visitor to the churchyard the
opportunity of walking along the parapets. The same is
true of the Wexford town wall near the western gate, close
to St Selskar's Church. Clonmel in County Tipperary
recently made great efforts to restore parts of its town walls.
But only about eight miles north is the county's — but also
the country's — best-kept town wall secret in the form of
the small town of Fethard. It is an absolute gem, retaining
its medieval churches and tower-houses — and a well-
preserved and recently conserved stretch of wall, as well as
a town gate through which no funeral will pass — as that
was the way Cromwell entered when he took the town in
1650. The tower-houses in Fethard are comparative
rarities. Most of the houses within the walls of a medieval
Irish town would have been made of wood, largely only
one floor high, but sometimes they were two-storeyed,
half-timbered houses, occupying most of the width of the
long narrow family plots of land which fronted on to the
streets. The tradesmen would have offered their wares in
front of the houses, and we know of many trades practised
in these towns, some of which have left their mark in still-
existing street names — carpenters, potters, leather
skinners, cloth weavers and dyers, coopers, and many more.

But gates standing alone in places like Fore in
County Westmeath or in a field at Trim, on the opposite
side of the river from the castle, remind us that there are
a number of medieval towns which have not survived as
viable economic entities and others which have been
totally deserted, leaving little to be seen above ground
except a few low earthen walls.

But the most impressive Irish town wall of all is that of the city of Derry, built by the London guilds who gave their name to town and county in the second decade of the seventeenth century. By largely removing traces of an earlier settlement, the builders were able to erect a whole new town on what was virtually a virgin site and, unlike the alleyways of some other Irish medieval towns such as Kilkenny, the streets were laid out on a regular grid pattern. The whole was enclosed within the most resplendent set of town walls on the whole island which, by the time they were completed in 1620, were among the last great set of such defences to be built anywhere in Europe. One of the great pleasures of visiting this noble city is a walk along the broad parapets of the wall and encountering the occasional cannon of a kind which would have been used in defence of many an Irish town centuries ago, but which have now become a rarity.

Blossom Gate, Kilmallock, Co. Limerick

Effigies of Knights, Ladies and Bishops

Death may be the great leveller but, even in its wake, many want to show that they are more equal than others by having grandiose monuments built to themselves and their memory. This, however, is no bad thing, for many a stone sculptor has thereby been given the opportunity of producing a masterpiece which has contributed to the treasury of medieval Irish art.

It was the Norman invaders who introduced to Ireland the idea of having an effigy carved to commemorate the deceased. Probably the best-known example of their zeal in this respect is the recumbent knight in Christ Church Cathedral, Dublin, known as 'Strongbow' — the mightiest of the Norman barons to set foot on Irish soil and the one who inherited the kingdom of Leinster by marrying the daughter of King Diarmait MacMurrough. But, as it happens, the effigy's fame and reputation is slightly misplaced because the coat of arms on the shield shows the armoured figure to have been not Strongbow but a rather obscure FitzOsbert knight carved probably more than a century after Strongbow's death.

It is again the coat of arms on the shield which helps us to identify as a member of the Cantwell family the superb thirteenth-century effigy at Kilfane, Co. Kilkenny — an over-lifesize figure of a knight in his full panoply, with a lordly and distinguished bearing. Who would not quiver before such might and strength which conquered the best of the Irish lands? But these haughty men had a tender side, too, and erected monuments bearing figures of what we may take to have been their beloved wives — even if they frequently omitted to inscribe their names.

Thus, we have a number of fine but anonymous portraits of thirteenth-century Norman ladies at places such as Christ Church Cathedral in Dublin, Grey Abbey, Co. Down, and in the grounds of the Protestant cathedral at Cashel, Co. Tipperary. Only rarely during the Anglo-Norman period were man and wife portrayed side by side, as was the case with the presumed pair of Butlers at Gowran, Co. Kilkenny, or the couple sharing a common stone on the attractively incised slab at Athassel in the neighbouring county of Tipperary.

After the country had begun to recover from the worst effects of the Black Death of 1348–50, which had decimated the Norman population and virtually annihilated the impetus to immortalise its dead in stone, the spirit rekindled two generations later among those of their fifteenth-century descendants who had, as the phrase went, become more Irish than the Irish themselves. It was in the Hiberno-Norman lands of Leinster that the rust was scraped from the sculptor's chisel and its edge resharpened to carve updated versions of the earlier effigies. But here greater respect was paid to the wives. The Plunket family in their Meath churches at Killeen, Rathmore and Dunsany, the St Lawrences at Howth in County Dublin, the FitzEustaces in Dublin and at Kilcullen, Co. Kildare but, above all, the Butlers in Kilkenny, had dignified memorials carved in memory of the knights and ladies of their families, often with extensive inscriptions identifying both of them. The difference between these and the earlier Norman effigies was not only the change in type of armour worn by the men, or the latest fashion in clothes and head-dress displayed by the women, but the fact that the effigies were laid on top of a box-tomb, the sides of which were ornamented with armorial bearings,

Crucifixion scenes and so called 'weepers' in the form of
apostle figures. The best collection of fifteenth/sixteenth-
century effigies of knights and ladies, both singly and
combined, is undoubtedly in St Canice's Cathedral in
Kilkenny, where the double-tomb of Piers Butler, the
Eighth Earl of Ormond, and his wife Margaret FitzGerald,
and the adjacent knight probably to be identified as his
successor James, the Ninth Earl, are particularly
noteworthy. But it should be pointed out that the sides of
the box-tombs presently supporting these and other
effigies in the cathedral are not necessarily those which
originally bore them, but rather the bits and pieces
collected up from what survived after Cromwell and his
men had wrought havoc inside the cathedral in 1650.

Throughout the later Middle Ages the native Irish did
not entirely stand idly by as the Normans made all the
running in tomb sculpture. In the northern half of County
Clare, for instance, a small band of stone sculptors were
trying to keep the flame alive by carving effigies of local
dignitaries, though admittedly not to the highest of
standards. In the chancel of Corcomroe Abbey, near the
northern end of the Burren, there is the recumbent effigy
of *c*.1300, said to be that of an O'Brien king killed near-by
in 1267. In the last century, it was thought that the carved
figure held a pipe in his hand, kindling notions of the Irish
having been among the earliest smokers in Europe, but it
transpired that all the royal fingers were doing was clasping
the cord of a cloak which the figure carried on his back.

In the wall above where this O'Brien figure rests there
is an unfinished effigy of the fourteenth century, this time
of an ecclesiastic, presumably the abbot of the Cistercian
monastery, who may have been a rough contemporary of
the bishop so attractively if naively incised on a slab in the

chancel of Kilfenora Cathedral not far away. The latter's
crozier is not state of the art, but a time-honoured
reliquary in the old Irish style, with three knops on the
stem, reminding one of the caricature boa constrictor
which has swallowed three balls. By the fifteenth century,
the quality of the Clare sculptors had improved greatly, as
can be seen in the fine tomb-surrounds in Ennis friary
which must have been imitating English alabaster tables
imported into Ireland from Nottingham.

Perhaps the noblest of all the Irish effigies is that of
Bishop Walter Wellesly (1539), formerly at Great Connell
in County Kildare where he was prior, but which was
moved in 1971 to Kildare Cathedral where he presided
as Bishop for the last decade of his life. This is the
monument of a patrician prelate, gentle and dignified,
unruffled by the tremors of the Reformation. The
patterned Italianate velvet of his chasuble shines through
as an artistic high point of the Irish Middle Ages, and the
bishop as a precursor of a Renaissance which, however,
was only marginally to affect the art of an Ireland torn by
bloody religious wars.

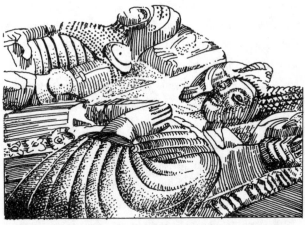

Double-effigy, St Canice's Cathedral, Kilkenny

Medieval Domestic Buildings

When you come to think of it, what has come down to us in the way of buildings from the later Middle Ages, apart from churches, castles and tower-houses? Precious little really. What about the common man or the common woman (or were they all uncommon?) — what did they live in, as not everyone could be a king in his own castle? Indeed, medieval Irish kings themselves didn't even live in castles. One English Cistercian abbot, Stephen of Lexington, somewhat deprecatingly described Irish 'kings' in 1228 as living in huts made of wattle. An Irish poet of around 1300 was much more magnanimous (if possibly a trifle over-blown) in describing the house of his royal master, Hugh O'Conor, King of Connacht, which was obviously of wood and surrounded by some earthworks. 'Spaciously palatial, smooth, with round pinnacles . . . the shapely fort of burnished doors . . . festive, glistening with drinking horns . . . a graceful ornamental pile . . . wood at hand for its buildings' are just some of the words used in his encomium. Probably those people further down the social scale would have had correspondingly simpler dwellings, perhaps rectangular with stone wall fittings of the kind found in excavations carried out at Caherguillamore in County Limerick over fifty years ago. But the serfs who tilled the land, yet owned none of it, would — because they were so often on the move — have had only the most makeshift of homes made out of twigs, or earth, or turf, or whatever other material might most easily have come to hand.

The first birds' eye views of Irish houses which have come down to us are no earlier than about 1600. These are preserved in a set of maps prepared by an English cartographer, Richard Barthelet, who was obviously a part of the Elizabethan military establishment in the north of Ireland. His drawings show a variety of one-roomed houses, rectangular in plan or with slightly curving walls made probably of earth, sods or wattle, covered with thatch and with gabled or hipped roofs — not very far removed from the thatched country house or cottage of today. Some of them would have been much the same size as their modern counterparts, but others would have been considerably smaller, like the *bothán scóir* inhabited by the humble labourer down to the last century, and reconstructed some years ago in the folk park at Bunratty.

But if we do go out hunting for medieval domestic buildings of stone other than tower-houses or those forming part of medieval order monasteries, we will not be entirely disappointed, and it is worthwhile making the effort to discover the rare examples. It is, however, not surprising that most of them were built by the medieval Irish clergy who, it should be pointed out, were never particularly affluent, nor indeed always paragons of priestly virtue. Some of the churches in Leinster, particularly the ones built by individual aristocratic families such as the Plunkets of Rathmore, Co. Meath, or those constructed to serve one of the richer settlements such as Newcastle Lyons in west Dublin, had multi-storey towers at the western end to house the clergy. St Doulagh's Church, on the Dublin–Malahide road, has a building history stretching over a period of 700 years, and bang in the middle of it is a central battlemented tower which almost certainly acted as living quarters for the clerics who administered the sacraments in the church.

Thousands have passed through the round-arched entrance gateway to the ecclesiastical ruins at Glendalough in County Wicklow without realising that above the arch there must have been at least one further floor, the wooden planks of which would have been supported on the internal corbels. This must surely have been the quarters of one or more priests whose job it was to oversee those entering the area of the sacred ruins of Glendalough, having trudged their way across the hills along St Kevin's Road. A similar function was probably fulfilled by a three-storey residential tower close to the church at Banagher in County Derry.

Almost more a 'palace' than a tower is the so called 'Glebe House' at Kilmacduagh, County Galway's 'Glendalough of the West', where a striking two-storey structure may have been built to house the abbot some distance away from the remarkable collection of churches on this venerable Irish monastic site. Looking more like the two-storey country house of today, however, is what is known as the 'Priest's House' or 'St Brendan's House' at Kilmalkedar, a stone's throw away from the famous Romanesque church located along the Saint's Road overlooking Smerwick Harbour near the end of the Dingle Peninsula. More down to earth are the stone houses with but a single floor at Temple Brecan close to the western end of Inis Mór, the largest of the three Aran islands in Galway Bay. What unites all of these buildings — Glendalough, Banagher, Kilmacduagh, Kilmalkedar and Temple Brecan — is that they were all located at centres of pilgrimage. We would, perhaps, not go too far wrong in seeing all of these unusual stone houses as the dwelling of the priests whose duty it would have been to oversee the pilgrimage traffic and officiate in religious ceremonies at the shrines, and no one would be too surprised if it turned out that it became possible to construct these houses largely thanks to the offerings of the pilgrims who must have come to venerate whichever saint's relics were preserved on site, and to seek a cure for whatever may have ailed them.

It was almost certainly thanks to churchmen too that another oft-neglected kind of medieval stone building was constructed strongly enough to last down to our own day, and that is the college, used for religious and educational purposes. The most extensive and impressive example is that on the Hill of Slane, but most of the revellers enjoying themselves in the Abbey Tavern in Howth are probably blissfully unaware that a building right next door to them is also a sixteenth-century college.

Towns, of course, had their domestic buildings. Those excavated in Dublin proved to be wooden post-and-wattle houses with squared timber doorways. Dalkey, Co. Dublin, Ardglass, Co. Down and Fethard, Co. Tipperary, automatically spring to mind as good examples of where urban domestic dwellings could also be of the tower-house variety. However, the town of Kilkenny preserves one stone building which is not a tower, but a fine town-house of the Elizabethan period — Rothe House on Parliament Street, built by John Rothe in 1594. It provides 'the marble city' with a touch of the Renaissance, having arcades on either side of the doorway, an oriel window above looking on to the street, and a passage leading into not one but two courtyards behind. Beautifully restored by the Kilkenny Archaeological Society during the last three decades, it now houses a museum of delights, not least of which is the well-preserved collection of theatrical costumes of the last two and a half centuries.

Medieval Friaries

If the Cistercians were the major European monastic
order founding houses in Ireland in the twelfth century,
other important orders followed in their footsteps a
hundred years later. These were the mendicant friars who
had taken vows of poverty and whose vocation it was to
preach the gospel and move among the people to help
them keep the faith in the often corrupt atmosphere of
later medieval Ireland. Two of these orders had only
recently been founded in Italy, the Franciscans and the
Dominicans, whereas the Carmelites had come west from
Palestine in the backwash of the Crusades.

The other important mendicant order in Ireland,
the Augustinians, had a longer history, having been
recognised officially in the middle of the eleventh century
— and they preceded the mendicant friars by a century,
having arrived at roughly the same time as the
Cistercians. The Augustinians founded their own houses
in Ireland, but were also introduced into some of the
older Irish monasteries such as Glendalough so as to
breathe new life into them, and thus enable them to
continue to function for a few centuries more than they
might otherwise have done.

It is noteworthy how the first foundations of the
important mendicant orders in Ireland tended to be in the
Norman towns, as it was there that they could get not
only the right kind of political patronage, but also an
audience for their sermons, and alms-givers to keep them
alive. Like the Cistercians, the Franciscans, too, were
divided in their political loyalties, some tending more
towards the Normans, others towards the Irish. One of

the latter's friaries was Ennis, which was founded by the
O'Brien family in the thirteenth century. The chancel is as
fine an example as one can get of the tall lancet windows
used in these friaries in the thirteenth and early fourteenth
centuries, other examples being Buttevant, Co. Cork, and
Ardfert, Co. Kerry.

The typical Franciscan friary had a long church,
standing (as with the Cistercians) on one side of the
cloister garth, around the other three sides of which
were ranged the domestic buildings — refectory, kitchen,
dormitory etc. The most characteristic features of these
friaries is the tall and slender tower which rises skywards
close to the middle of the hall-like church, and also the
latter's traceried east window, which shows a considerable
variety and commendable standard of workmanship.
Indeed, the Franciscan friaries in particular are among
the finest achievements of late medieval ecclesiastical
architecture in Ireland.

The Black Death of 1347–50 took a considerable toll
on the communities of friars within the walls of Norman
towns, where the bubonic plague had raged most fiercely.
During the fifteenth century, however, the trend was very
much more towards building the friaries out in the
countryside, particularly among the rural-based Gaelic
population in the western half of Ireland. But, as the later
Middle Ages progressed, secularisation became more
rampant and the necessity to instil new vigour into the
religious way of life led to the introduction of the
Observantine reform which — as its name implies — was
designed to observe and stick more closely to the rules laid
down by the founding saints. This reform movement
started among the Franciscans in Quin, Co. Clare, but
spread rapidly among other existing houses and was the

basis of the rule of many of the new houses founded in the
fifteenth century.

Fine examples of this Franciscan architecture can be
found at Adare in County Limerick (in the midst of the
local golf course), Askeaton in the same county, Muckross
near Killarney, Kilconnell, Claregalway and Ross Errilly
in County Galway, Kilcrea, Co. Cork, as well as at
Rosserk and Moyne in County Mayo. What a number of
these have in common is the universally well-preserved
cloister arcading which, unlike the Cistercian lean-to
buildings of the same kind, actually support the domestic
rooms on the first floor. Some of the friaries, such as
Askeaton and Ennis, feature a sculpture of St Francis
bearing his stigmata, and Creevelea, near Dromahair in
County Leitrim, has, in addition, a representation of the
saint talking to the birds whose language he is said to
have understood.

The Dominican order concentrated somewhat more
on preaching than did the Franciscans, but they both
had the same long, halled church, and shared the same
tall, narrow tower almost halfway along its length. The
friary at Kilmallock, Co. Limerick, founded near the end
of the thirteenth century, gives us the best impression of
what one of these medieval Dominican friaries was like
in its heyday and, in addition, provides us with some
good-quality carved heads. But there are many others —
Aghaboe, Co. Laois, Athenry and Portumna in Co.
Galway, Carlingford, Co. Louth, Lorrha and Cashel in
County Tipperary, as well as Sligo town and Urlaur in
the neighbouring county of Mayo, where the churches
are fairly well preserved. Another has recently been
revealed by the archaeologist's spade in the centre of
Cork city.

The Augustinian friars, otherwise known as the
Austin friars, have the distinction of having two of their
foundations numbered among the handful of medieval
churches — as opposed to cathedrals — which are still in
use in Ireland. One of these is in Fethard, Co. Tipperary,
where the original friary, founded in 1306, was — like
so many religious foundations — dissolved at the
Reformation around 1540, but the friars were able to
return in 1820 and restore their ancient church so that it
could function once more as a Catholic church, which it
still does. A somewhat different, though equally fortunate
fate befell the Augustinian friary church, commonly
known as the Black Abbey, at Adare in County Limerick.
It had been founded early in the fourteenth century, but
long after the Reformation it was lucky enough to have
come into the hands of the Wyndham-Quin family, Earls
of Dunraven, who did so much to make Adare one of the
great medieval showpieces of Ireland. They made the
Black Abbey into their family mausoleum and restored the
fabric to its former glory as the local Church of Ireland
church so that, in many respects, it remains much the same
as it was during the late Middle Ages. Another of the
churches which benefited greatly from the Dunraven
generosity was the only Irish house of the Trinitarian
Canons which the family restored and gave over to the
Catholic Church in 1811, so that it now serves as the
Catholic church in the village of Adare. Two medieval
churches still in splendid condition and each used by a
different denomination for divine service in one and the
same village is certainly something of a record for Ireland.

But some of the other orders already mentioned also
have medieval churches which are still in use. The
Franciscans, for instance, have very successfully restored

their church at Multyfarnham in County Westmeath,
and their church at Meelick, close to the River Shannon
in County Galway, is another all too seldomly visited
example. The Dominicans brought to life again what had
been little more than a skeleton at the Black Abbey in
Kilkenny city. Finally, one may mention the abbey church
at Ballintober, Co. Mayo, founded for the Augustinian
Canons in 1216 by Cathal Crovdearg, King of Connacht,
and, despite great vicissitudes for centuries after the
Reformation, it was beautifully restored and reopened for
Catholic church services to commemorate 750 years of its
existence in 1966. Though few in number, there are more
medieval friaries and priories still in use in Ireland than
one might imagine. But even when not restored, the
others are well worth a visit as being among the most
atmospheric buildings of the later Middle Ages in Ireland.

Ross Errilly Friary, Co. Galway

Tower-houses

'We are come to the castle already. The castles are built very strong with narrows stayres [stairs] for security. The hall is the uppermost room, lett us go up, you shall not come down again till tomorrow.'

Thus an English commentator, Luke Gernon, described his first impressions on entering an Irish castle in 1620. We do not know which castle he had been visiting but, except for the bit about 'not coming down again till tomorrow', he could well have been talking about Bunratty Castle today, where medieval banquets are re-enacted there in the evenings. These festivities also bring to life more of Gernon's remarks about how guests were received in a medieval Irish castle:

'Salutations paste, you shall be presented with all the drinks in the house . . . the table is spread and plentifully furnished with variety of meates . . . they feast together with great jollyty and healths around; towards the middle of the supper, the harper begins to tune and singeth Irish rhymes of auncient making . . .'

Bunratty Castle, cleverly built beside the road to Shannon Airport as one tourist put it, is one of those thousands of 'castles' which sprang up over many parts of Ireland during the fifteenth and sixteenth centuries, though it must be said that few are as imposing, and none as well furnished, as Bunratty, which was built by the MacNamara family around 1450 and later came into O'Brien hands. Another well-known example raised at around the same

time, and on the same impressive scale, is Blarney Castle,
erected by Cormac 'the Strong' MacCarthy in 1446 and
housing that most famous 'stone of eloquence' said to give
you 'the gift of the gab' if you kiss it whilst lying on your
back 85 feet (26m) above the ground.

But the majority of these late medieval Irish castles
are rather more modest in size, consisting of one room
per floor and linked vertically together by a spiral
staircase. A typical example would be rectangular in
ground plan, have four or five floors, the lowermost and
occasionally one other being vaulted over with a stone
roof. A splendid cross-section of just what the inside of
one of these tower-houses looked like is provided by
Carrigafoyle Castle in north Kerry where half of the
castle has conveniently collapsed to reveal its interior.
Entrance is by a single door leading to a passage with a
murder hole above, through which the inhabitants could
throw down stones or missiles on hapless intruders. As
Gernon indicated, the main 'hall' where the castle-owner
lived was on the top floor, protected from the elements
by a stout oak roof covered with slates, his winter
evenings sometimes warmed by blazing logs in a large
fireplace, and his view over the surrounding countryside
assured by one or more pairs of windows. To protect
himself and his family from rapacious neighbours, he
might also have a projecting machicolation above
ground-floor level from which he could pour scorn and
boiling water or throw missiles upon the unwelcome.
Sometimes, small holes in the walls show that provision
was made for the use of musket-fire against the unwanted
enemy. Bawns outside, protected by high stone walls,
provided further defences and protection for cattle and
sheep in the evening.

Nowadays, 'castles' is the word we use to describe
these buildings, which are more correctly termed 'tower-
houses' or 'tower-house castles'. For houses they were, the
homes of the more affluent Gaelic and Anglo-Norman
families who wanted to show off their wealth as much as
they wanted to defend themselves when the state was not
interested in offering them protection. They were able to
afford the building of these towers by making their poor
tenants provide for the construction team of carpenters
and masons. These tower-houses are the most numerous
and noticeable stone monuments of the later Middle Ages
in Ireland, as they lord it over the surrounding landscape,
particularly in flattish areas of the country such as east
Galway. It is there, incidentally, that we find the most
literary of all tower-houses, Thoor Ballylee near Gort,
which the poet W. B. Yeats made his occasional home
from about 1917 till 1926.

Thoor Ballylee looks out over a stream, and water
provides the backdrop for some of the most picturesque
tower-houses in the country — Narrow Water Castle,
between Warrenpoint and Rostrevor in County Down,
Doe Castle on Sheephaven Bay, Co. Donegal, Ross Castle
on the lakes of Killarney, Dun Guaire on Galway Bay,
Kildavnet on Achill Island and Ferrycarrig on the banks of
the Slaney estuary in County Wexford. Ardee, Co. Louth,
Ardglass, Co. Down and Dalkey, Co. Dublin, show how
such towers could be built in a purely urban context,
providing homes and warehousing for the wealthier
merchants, and Lynch's Castle in Galway city (now an
AIB bank) is the most ornate example of such a tower-
house located in the setting of a medieval Irish town.

The only Irish tower-house to have retained part of
its original wooden roof is Dunsoghly, Co. Dublin, which

served as a model for the reconstructed roof at Bunratty. The Office of Public Works has made great strides in re-roofing other important castles such as Cahir, Co. Tipperary, or Aughnanure, Co. Galway, but private interests have also shown enthusiasm in restoring tower-houses which they open at certain times to the public, as at Redwood, Co. Tipperary, or Newtown, near Ballyvaughan, Co. Clare, the latter unusual in being one of a rare breed of round tower-houses.

How or when these tower-houses developed, and who first built them, are questions which have yet to be solved satisfactorily in the absence of historical sources about most of them. The likelihood is gradually increasing that they may have first started in the late fourteenth century, taking their inspiration perhaps from the smaller specimens of the earlier Norman castles, but they were most popular in the fifteenth and sixteenth centuries, though occasionally still being built in the seventeenth. But, at that stage, the more commodious manor house with bigger windows and less protection was beginning to replace the narrow arrow-slits and threatening defences of the tower-houses — a contrast strikingly illustrated in the juxtaposition at Leamaneh, Co. Clare, of the introspective tower-house and the enlightened manor beckoning to a more gracious lifestyle as the Middle Ages receded more and more into the historical past.

Plantation Castles

T hroughout the whole medieval period, Gaelic Ulster had held its head high and free, but everything was to change with the Elizabethan conquest and the subsequent departure of the flower of the province's nobility in 1607. The door was opened to a flood of new immigrants from Scotland and England who were to change the face and the spirit of northern Ireland, as well as the pattern of landownership.

The various guilds or companies of the city of London were given a whole new county to themselves, to which their name was attached — Londonderry. They set about building towns such as Derry and Coleraine, but the half-timbered houses which they built there have long since disappeared. There were also many privateers in the other counties of Ulster who got grants of land on condition that they attract other immigrants across the Irish Sea to come and settle. But, surrounded by a Gaelic population who had been the owners of the lands they now occupied, these Planters had a need to defend themselves, which they did by building castles and bawns for themselves and their families.

Bawns were walled enclosures, square or rectangular in shape and with towers at some, if not all, of the corners — from which muskets could be fired at an approaching enemy. A simple example can be found at Brackfield, about six miles from Derry and overlooking the road to Dungiven and Belfast. It was built by the Skinners' Company around 1615 and, in addition to the 10 foot (3m) high wall with a flanking tower at diagonally opposite ends, it has a ruined two-storey house built by

Sir Edward Doddington. Rather more impressive in its
dimensions — 110 x 130 feet (*c.* 34 x 39m) — and
dramatic in its siting on a cliff 120 feet (36m) above the
River Blackwater, is a bawn built around 1611 by Sir
Richard Wingfield at Benburb, near where Owen Roe
O'Neill was to defeat the Ulster Scots in 1646. Square
and round towers on its periphery show its military intent,
but it is now a haven of peace in the grounds of a Servite
priory. Smaller but more imposing defences can be seen
on the roadway side of the bawn built by John Dalway
only a few miles north of Carrickfergus, Co. Antrim,
around 1609.

   Similar bawns were used as the first form of
obstruction erected against those who might try to get
into the much taller stone castles which the Planters
built to protect themselves. Probably the most unusual in
appearance, but also one of the best preserved, is Monea,
some miles north-west of Enniskillen in County
Fermanagh. A long rectangle in plan, its entrance is
squeezed in between two rounded drum-towers which
look as if they have the walls of two cottages at right
angles to one another stranded on top of them. But they
were just part of the living quarters of Malcolm Hamilton
who built the castle around 1618–19 and who, at the
other end, added turrets supported by corbels — a feature
found on much Plantation architecture of the seventeenth
century and always a give-away for the Scottish origin of
its builders. These corbels are frequently found in Scotland
even as late as the nineteenth century where they are a
most typical feature of the architectural style we have
come to know as 'Scottish baronial'.

   Close to Monea is another castle, roughly
contemporary in date, but with a bloody history attached

to it. This is Tully, built by Sir John Hume before 1619,
and consisting of a T-shaped two-storeyed castle (with
vaulted ground floor) and a bawn which has largely
disappeared. Sir John, who hailed from Berwickshire,
died in 1639, and two years later the castle was besieged
by Rory Maguire, who was the former owner of the lands
on which the castle had been built. Rory attacked on
Christmas Eve, when most of the men were away and the
castle was filled largely with women and children. Lady
May Hume surrendered in the belief that she had been
assured a safe conduct. She and her direct family were
spared, but not the remaining sixty women and children
and fifteen men who were put to the sword. The castle
was never inhabited again, but today its peace has returned
and the partially cobbled bawn has been converted into a
garden with plants of the kind that would have been
assembled there in the seventeenth century. The castle
stands on a hillock overlooking Lough Erne and is an
attractive spot approachable by land and water.

By a fortunate coincidence, many of the surviving
pieces of Plantation architecture are located close to water,
which adds to their visual attractiveness. Overlooking
Lough Gill, just on the Leitrim side of the Sligo border,
is Newtown, better known as Parke's Castle, recently
splendidly restored inside by the Office of Public Works.
Built around the 1620s by Captain Robert Parke, it
replaced a tower-house held by the O'Rourkes of Breifne,
who offered shelter there to Francisco de Cuellar, the only
Spaniard to have recorded personally the nightmarish
experiences of a Spanish Armada shipwreck. Instead of
being knocked down, the O'Donnell tower-house in
Donegal town was used and added to at around the same
time by Sir Basil Brooke, who inserted a swaggering

chimney-piece on the first floor of the old tower while
building a Jacobean-style mansion next door. This castle,
along with Parke's, Ardtarmon Castle in Sligo and a little-
known example at Robertstown in County Meath, are
among the few examples of Plantation architecture
surviving in the Republic.

The Watergate in Enniskillen, giving on to the
River Erne beside the castle, is another good example of
the aquatic location of Plantation architecture in Scottish
baronial style. But the most welcoming of all, and one
of the few to be still inhabited, is away at the other (east)
end of the province — at Ballygalley, where the Glens of
Antrim meet the sea. With its corbelled corner turrets,
and conical roofs like candle-snuffers, it is still actively
functioning as part of a fine modern hotel, and thus gives
us a better idea than any other Plantation castle what such
buildings must have looked like when comparatively new.
Built by James Shaw of Greenock on the Clyde in 1625, it
is very Scottish in appearance and looks out over the short
stretch of sea to the Mull of Kintyre and the Rhins of
Galloway, reminding us that all of those Scottish settlers
who participated in the Ulster Plantations of the early
seventeenth century did not have very far to come and
make themselves a home from home.

Ballygalley Castle Hotel, Co. Antrim

Post-medieval Fortifications

Medieval castles were erected largely to retain land conquered by the Norman barons or to impress on neighbours the importance of the man who built a tower-house in a particular locality. By a curious turn-around of fate, the large post-medieval fortifications were built not to contain enemies within the country, but to prevent foes entering Ireland from outside.

Bearing in mind the traumatic prospect that the Spanish Armada could conceivably have been a success, had the weather and other circumstances been kinder to King Philip's 'Grand Enterprise', the English government was afraid of a sea-borne army invading Ireland particularly from the south, and using it then as a backdoor to England. Throughout the seventeenth and eighteenth centuries, the south coast in particular was fitted out with a series of batteries which could fire on an approaching squadron. Prime survivor of such maritime defences is Charles Fort, south of Kinsale, a tremendous star-shaped fort built during the reign of Charles II (1660–85), after whom it was named.

During the following century, the centre of naval fortification moved from Kinsale to Cork Harbour, where the batteries such as Spike Island look particularly threatening from the sea. Waterford Harbour was another safe inlet which was always under potential threat of invasion, but it was well protected from Duncannon Fort which stands in a position of strength on the Wexford side of the inlet.

Efforts by the French to land in Ireland did once turn out to be successful when General Humbert landed

in Killala in 1796, and, with the rebellion two years later
of the United Irishmen who had been in close contact
with France in the aftermath of the Revolution, England
once more became worried about a possible invasion from
France. When the nineteenth century dawned, the
emphasis turned from the south coast to two parallel
north-south axes — the east coast on the one hand, and
the Shannon River on the other. Within the first two
decades of the new century, the east coast was fortified
with a series of massive round towers called Martello
towers, it is alleged, after a similar tower at a place called
Mortella on the island of Corsica which the English had
found to be impregnable. These towers were carefully
placed in such a way that they were always in sight of their
immediate neighbours, so that north and south of Dublin
a message could be passed speedily to the capital city to
warn of any foreign fleet on the horizon. But the cannon
which were mounted on a swivel on the roof of each
tower were never used, as Napoleon never sent a navy to
Ireland. These towers, however, were by no means
confined to the east coast, and are also found sporadically
along other Irish shores.

The English government feared, too, that the French
could land somewhere along the west coast, as Humbert
had done, and so a series of fortifications were erected
along the western bank of the Shannon. By far the most
conspicuous of these are the extensive defences at
Shannonbridge, where even the modern motorist could
feel intimidated by the high walls on the roadside. But the
guns are silent there now — indeed, they were never fired
in anger from the towers as, once again, Napoleon denied
them the chance of ever taking a pot-shot at him or his
troops. His Waterloo was to come elsewhere.

Bibliography

Barrow, George Lennox, *The Round Towers of Ireland: A Study and Gazetteer* (Dublin 1979).

Bradley, John, *Walled Towns in Ireland* (Dublin 1995).

Craig, Maurice, *The Architecture of Ireland from the earliest times to 1880* (Dublin/London 1982).

Galloway, Peter, *The Cathedrals of Ireland* (Belfast 1992).

Harbison, Peter, *Pre-Christian Ireland* (London 1988).

Harbison, Peter, *Guide to the National and Historic Monuments of Ireland* (Dublin 1992).

Harbison, Peter, *Irish High Crosses with the figure sculpture explained* (Drogheda 1994).

Herity, Michael, *Irish Passage Graves* (Dublin 1974).

Hughes, Kathleen and Ann Hamlin, *The Modern Traveller to the Early Irish Church* (London 1977).

Hunt, John, *Irish Medieval Figure Sculpture, 1200–1600* (Dublin/London 1974).

Johnson, David Newman, *The Irish Castle,* The Irish Heritage Series (Dublin 1985).

Kerrigan, Paul, *Castles and Fortifications in Ireland, 1485–1945* (Cork 1995).

Leask, H.G., *Irish Castles and Castellated Houses* (Dundalk 1941; oft reprinted).

Leask, H.G., *Irish Churches and Monastic Buildings,* 3 vols (Dundalk 1955–60; oft reprinted).

MacManus, Damian, *A Guide to Ogam,* Maynooth Monographs (Maynooth 1991).

Manning, Conleth, *Early Irish Monasteries* (Dublin 1995).

O'Brien, Jacqueline and Peter Harbison, *Ancient Ireland* (London/New York 1996).

Ó Nualláin, Seán, *Stone Circles in Ireland* (Dublin 1995).

Petrie, George, 'The ecclesiastical architecture of Ireland, anterior to the Norman Anglo-Irish invasion; comprising an essay on the origin and uses of the Round Towers of Ireland', Transactions of the Royal Irish Academy 20, 1845, 1–521.

Raftery, Barry, *Pagan Celtic Ireland: The Enigma of the Irish Iron Age* (London 1994).

Stalley, Roger, *The Cistercian Monasteries of Ireland* (London/New Haven 1987).

Sweetman, David, *Irish Castles and Fortified Houses* (Dublin 1995).

Thomas, Avril, *The Walled Towns of Ireland,* 2 vols (Blackrock 1992).

Twohig, Elizabeth Shee, *Irish Megalithic Tombs,* Shire Archaeology Series (Princes Risborough 1990).

Westrop, Thomas Johnson, 'The ancient forts of Ireland', Transactions of the Royal Irish Academy 31, 1901, 579–72.

Index to Place Names

Achill Island, Co. Galway, 85
Adare, Co. Limerick, 63, 80, 81
Aghaboe, Co. Laois, 80
Aghadoe, Co. Kerry, 50
Ahenny, Co. Tipperary, 43
Antrim, Co. Antrim, 45
Aran Islands, Co. Galway, 23–4, 76
Arboe, Co. Tyrone, 42
Ardagh chalice, 28
Ardee, Co. Louth, 85
Ardfert, Co. Kerry, 27, 50, 58, 61, 79
Ardglass, Co. Down, 77, 85
Ardmore, Co. Waterford, 27, 47, 51, 61
Ardtarmon Castle, Co. Sligo, 90
Armagh, Co. Armagh, 29, 43, 60
Askeaton, Co. Limerick, 80
Athassel, Co. Tipperary, 71
Athenry, Co. Galway, 65, 67, 80
Athlone Castle, Co. Westmeath, 65
Aughnacliff, Co. Longford, 14
Aughnanure, Co. Galway, 86

Ballintober, Co. Mayo, 82
Ballintubber, Co. Roscomon, 65
Ballyferriter, Co. Kerry, 39
Ballygalley, Co. Antrim, 90
Ballymote, Co. Sligo, 64
Ballynoe, Co. Down, 19
Baltinglass, Co. Wicklow, 55
Banagher, Co. Derry, 76
Bangor, Co. Down, 31
Beaghmore, Co. Tyrone, 19
Beltany, Co. Donegal, 12, 18
Benburb, Co. Tyrone, 88
Blarney Castle, Co. Cork, 84
Boa Island, Lough Erne, 21
Boyle Abbey, Co. Roscommon, 54–55, 57
Brackfield, Co. Derry, 87–8
Brewel, Co. Wicklow, 16
Bullaun, Co. Galway, 20
Bunratty, Co. Clare, 75, 83, 86
Burren, Co. Clare, 15, 24, 25, 55–6, 61, 72
Buttevant, Co. Cork, 79

Caherballykinvarga, Co. Clare, 24

Cahercommaun, Co. Clare, 24–5
Caherguillamore, Co. Limerick, 74
Cahermacnaghten, Co. Clare, 25
Cahir, Co. Tipperary, 86
Caldragh, Co. Fermanagh, 21
Carlingford, Co. Louth, 64, 80
Carlow, Co. Carlow, 65
Carrickfergus, Co. Antrim, 63, 65, 88
Carrigafoyle Castle, Co. Kerry, 84
Carrigogunnell, Co. Limerick, 64
Carrowkeel, Co. Sligo, 12
Carrowmore, Co. Sligo, 11–12, 13, 14, 18
Cashel, Co. Tipperary, 44, 49–50, 61, 71, 80
Castle Archdale, Lough Erne, 21
Castlebernard, Co. Offaly, 43
Castleknock, Co. Dublin, 64
Castlestrange, Co. Roscommon, 21
Charles Fort, Co. Cork, 91
Church Island, Co. Kerry, 27, 39
Claregalway, Co. Galway, 80
Clonard, Co. Meath, 31
Clondalkin, Co. Dublin, 45
Clonfert, Co. Galway, 52, 58
Clonmacnoise, Co. Offaly, 31, 32, 38–9, 42, 43, 48, 50, 52
Clonmel, Co. Tipperary, 68
Clough, Co. Down, 62
Cloyne Cathedral, Co. Cork, 60–61
Coleraine, Co. Derry, 87
Cong, Co. Mayo, 16–17
Corca Dhuibhne, 33
Corcomroe Abbey, Co. Clare, 55–6, 72
Cork, Co. Cork, 27, 80
Craggaunowen, Co. Clare, 22, 25
Creevelea, Co. Leitrim, 80
Croagh Patrick, Co. Mayo, 36

Dalkey, Co. Dublin, 77, 85
Derry, Co. Derry, 60, 69, 87
Derrykeighan, Co. Antrim, 21
Derrynaflan chalice, 28
Devenish, Co. Fermanagh, 31, 32, 45–6, 47

Dingle Peninsula, Co. Kerry, 27, 33, 36, 39, 76
Doe Castle, Co. Donegal, 85
Donaghmore, Co. Tyrone, 42
Donegal, Co. Donegal, 89–90
Downpatrick Cathedral, Co. Down, 60
Dowth, Co. Meath, 9
Drogheda, Co. Louth, 9, 67
Drombeg, Co. Cork, 18, 19
Drumlohan, Co. Waterford, 27
Dubh Cathair, Aran Islands, 24
Dublin, 56–7, 58–9, 63, 66, 70
Dun Aengus, Aran Islands, 23–4
Dun Ailinne, Co. Kildare, 30
Dun Guaire Castle, Co. Galway, 85
Dunamase Castle, Co. Laois, 64
Dunbrody Abbey, Co. Wexford, 56
Duncannon Fort, Co. Wexford, 91
Dundrum, Co. Down, 65
Dunloe, Co. Kerry, 27
Dunluce, Co. Antrim, 64
Dunsany, Co. Meath, 71
Dunsoghly, Co. Dublin, 85–6
Dysert O'Dea, Co. Clare, 44, 51

Ennis Friary, Co. Clare, 79
Enniskillen, Co. Fermanagh, 90

Fahan Mura, Co. Donegal, 37, 39
Ferns, Co. Wexford, 60–61, 65
Ferrycarrig, Co. Wexford, 22, 85
Fethard, Co. Tipperary, 68, 77, 81
Fore, Co. Westmeath, 68
Fourknocks, Co. Meath, 11
Freshford, Co. Kilkenny, 52

Gallarus Oratory, Co. Kerry, 35–6
Gallen, Co. Offaly, 39
Galway, Co. Galway, 85
Glasnevin Cemetery, Dublin, 45
Glen of Aherlow, Co. Tipperary, 39
Glendalough, Co. Wicklow, 31, 32, 39, 44–5, 48, 50, 76, 78
Gowran, Co. Kilkenny, 71
Graiguenamanagh, Co. Kilkenny, 56, 57
Grange, Co. Limerick, 18
Great Connell, Co. Kildare, 73
Grey Abbey, Co. Down, 55, 71
Grianán of Aileach, Co. Donegal, 23

Holy Cross, Co. Tipperary, 57
Hore Abbey, Co. Tipperary, 54
Howth, Co. Dublin, 71, 77

Inch, Co. Down, 55
Inis Mór, Aran Islands, 23–4, 76
Inisfallen, Co. Kerry, 50
Inisglora, Co. Mayo, 35
Inishcealtra, Co. Clare, 31, 39
Inishmurray, Co. Sligo, 31, 32
Iona, Outer Hebrides, 29
Isle of Man, 45

Jerpoint Abbey, Co. Kilkenny, 55

Kealkil, Co. Cork, 19
Kells, Co. Meath, 31, 32, 42, 44
Kilclooney, Co. Donegal, 14
Kilconnell, Co. Galway, 80
Kilcrea, Co. Cork, 80
Kilcullen, Co. Kildare, 71
Kildare, Co. Kildare, 45–6, 59, 73
Kildavnet, Achill Island, 85
Kilfane, Co. Kilkenny, 70
Kilfenora Cathedral, Co. Clare, 61, 73
Kilkenny, Co. Kilkenny, 45–6, 58, 60, 65, 69, 71–2, 73, 77, 82
Killala, Co. Mayo, 45, 92
Killaloe, Co. Clare, 50, 52, 60
Killarney, Co. Kerry, 17, 27
Killeen, Co. Meath, 71
Killeshin, Co. Laois, 51
Killycluggin, Co. Cavan, 21
Kilmacduagh, Co. Galway, 46, 76
Kilmalkedar, Co. Kerry, 27, 37, 50, 76
Kilmallock, Co. Limerick, 67, 69, 80
Kilmore, Co. Cavan, 51
Kilnasaggart, Co. Armagh, 37
Kilteel, Co. Kildare, 51
Kinsale, Co. Cork, 91
Knockmany, Co. Tyrone, 11, 12
Knocknarea, Co. Sligo, 12
Knowth, Co. Meath, 9, 10, 13

Leamaneh, Co. Clare, 86
Legananny, Co. Down, 14
Leighlin Cathedral, Co. Carlow, 60–61

Limerick, Co. Limerick, 61, 63
Lismore Cathedral, Co. Waterford,
    60–61
Lissyvigeen, Co. Kerry, 18, 19
London, 87
Londonderry, County, 87
Lorrha, Co. Tipperary, 80
Loughcrew, Co. Meath, 11
Lough Gur, Co. Limerick, 18
Lusk, Co. Dublin, 31

Maghera, Co. Derry, 51
Meelick, Co. Galway, 82
Mellifont, Co. Louth, 53, 54, 55, 56
Monaincha, Co. Tipperary, 52
Monasterboice, Co. Louth, 7, 41,
    42, 43, 44, 47
Monea, Co. Fermanagh, 88
Moone, Co. Kildare, 41
Mount Brandon, Co. Kerry, 34–5
Moyne, Co. Mayo, 80
Muckross, Co. Kerry, 80
Multyfarnham, Co. Westmeath, 82

Narrow Water Castle, Co. Down,
    85
National Museum of Ireland, 20,
    21, 27, 28
Navan Fort, Co. Armagh, 30
Nenagh Castle, Co. Tipperary, 65
Nendrum, Co. Down, 30, 39
Newcastle Lyons, Co. Dublin, 75
Newcastle West, Co. Limerick, 63
Newgrange, Co. Meath, 9–10, 12,
    13, 17–18
Newtown, Co. Clare, 86
Newtown, Co. Leitrim, 89, 90

Old Kilcullen, Co. Kildare, 30
Oldcastle, Co. Meath, 11
Omagh, Co. Tyrone, 22

Parke's Castle, Co. Leitrim, 89, 90
Piper's Stones, Co. Wicklow, 16
Portumna, Co. Galway, 80
Poulnabrone, Co. Clare, 15
Proleek, Co. Louth, 14

Quin, Co. Clare, 79

Raphoe, Co. Donegal, 51

Rathmore, Co. Meath, 71, 75
Redwood, Co. Tipperary, 86
Robertstown, Co. Meath, 90
Roche's Castle, Co. Louth, 63–4
Rock of Cashel, 44, 49–50, 61
Roscommon Castle, Co.
    Roscommon, 64–5
Roscrea, Co. Tipperary, 50, 65
Ross Castle, Co. Kerry, 85
Ross Errilly, Co. Galway, 80, 82
Rosserk, Co. Mayo, 80
Rothe House, Kilkenny, 77

St Doulagh's Church, Co. Dublin,
    75
St Mullins, Co. Carlow, 30
Saul, Co. Down, 39
Scattery Island, Co. Clare, 46
Seefin Mountain, Co. Wicklow, 11
Shanid, Co. Limerick, 65
Shannonbridge, 92
Skellig Michael, Co. Kerry, 31–2,
    36
Slane, Co. Meath, 77
Slea Head, Co. Kerry, 34
Sligo, Co. Sligo, 80
Spike Island, Co. Cork, 91
Staigue Fort, Co. Kerry, 23

Temple Brecan, Aran Islands, 76
Thoor Ballylee, Co. Galway, 85
Timahoe, Co. Laois, 6, 47
Toureen Peakaun, Co. Tipperary,
    39
Trim, Co. Meath, 62–3, 65, 68
Tuam, Co. Galway, 44, 52
Tully, Co. Fermanagh, 88–9
Tullylease, Co. Cork, 37–8
Turoe stone, Co. Galway, 20

Ulster History Park, Omagh, 22
Ulster Museum, Belfast, 21
Urlaur, Co. Mayo, 80

Ventry Harbour, Co. Kerry, 34–5

Waterford, Co. Waterford, 66–7
Wexford, Co. Wexford, 68
White Island, Lough Erne, 21

Youghal, Co. Cork, 68